Engaged
Spirituality

Engaged Spirituality

Ten Lives *of* Contemplation *and* Action

Janet W. Parachin

CHALICE
PRESS

ST. LOUIS, MISSOURI

Cover Design: Scott Tjaden
Interior Design: Wynn Younker
Art Director: Michael Domínguez

www.chalicepress.com

Print: 9780827208148
EPUB: 9780827208339 EPDF: 9780827208346

**Library of Congress Cataloging in Publication data
available upon request**

Printed in the United States of America

Contents

Introduction   1

1. Howard Thurman
    *Seeking Understanding among
    People of Different Faiths*   9

2. Simone Weil
    *To Live and Work as One
    of the Simple Folk*   22

3. Elie Wiesel
    That No One Should Ever Forget   34

4. Marian Wright Edelman
    All Children Are Our Children   48

5. Thich Nhat Hanh
    *Easing Suffering through
    Compassion for All*   63

6. Rigoberta Menchú
    *Champion of Indian Rights
    in Guatemala*   79

7. Vine Deloria, Jr.
    *Speaking Out for Native American
    Self-determination*   96

8. Joanna Macy
    At One with the Natural World   113

9. Rabindranath Tagore
    *Looking at the World with
    an Artist's Eyes*   129

10. Dorothy Day
    Seeing Christ in the Faces of the Poor   145

ACKNOWLEDGMENTS

From Simone Weil's *Formative Writings, 1929–1941,* translated and edited by Dorothy Tuck McFarland and Wilhelmina van Ness, published in Amherst in 1987 by the University of Massachusetts Press and copyrighted © 1987 by the University of Massachusetts Press. Used with permission.

From *Waiting for God* by Simone Weil, translated by Emma Craufurd, translation copyright 1951, renewed © 1979 by G.P. Putnam's Sons. Used by permission of G.P. Putnam's Sons, a division of Penguin Putnam Inc.

From *From the Kingdom of Memory* (New York: Summit Books, 1990). Copyright © 1990 by Elirion Associates, Inc. Reprinted by permission of Georges Borchardt, Inc. for the author.

From *Six Days of Destruction* by Elie Wiesel and Albert A. Friedlander. (Mahwah, N.J.: Paulist Press, 1988). Copyright © 1988 by Elirion Associates, Inc. & Central Conference of American Rabbis and Albert A. Friedlander. Originally appeared in The New Yorker. Reprinted by permission of Georges Borchardt, Inc. for the authors.

Reprinted from *A Jew Today* (1978) by Elie Wiesel with permission of Random House, Inc., New York, New York.

From *Families in Peril* by Marian Wright Edelman. Copyright © 1987 by the President and Fellows of Harvard College. Reprinted by permission of Harvard University Press.

From *Measure of Our Success* by Marian Wright Edelman. Copyright © 1992 by Marian Wright Edelman. Reprinted by permission of Beacon Press, Boston.

From *Guide My Feet* by Marian Wright Edelman. Copyright © 1995 by Marian Wright Edelman. Reprinted by permission of Beacon Press, Boston.

Reprinted from *Being Peace* (1987) by Thich Nhat Hanh with permission of Parallax Press, Berkeley, California.

Reprinted from *Touching Peace: Practicing the Art of Mindful Living* (1992) by Thich Nhat Hanh with permission of Parallax Press, Berkeley, California.

From *Living Buddha, Living Christ* by Thich Nhat Hanh. Copyright © 1995 by Thich Nhat Hanh. Used by permission of Putnam Berkley, a division of Penguin Putnam Inc.

Reprinted with the permission of Simon & Schuster, Inc. from *Popol Vuh* by Dennis Tedlock. Copyright © 1985 by Dennis Tedlock; copyright © renewed 1995 by Dennis Tedlock.

Reprinted with the permission of Simon & Schuster, Inc. from *Custer Died for Your Sins: An Indian Manifesto* by Vine Deloria, Jr. Copyright © 1969 by Vine Deloria, Jr.

Reprinted with the permission of Simon & Schuster, Inc. from *We Talk, You Listen: New Tribes,* New Turf by Vine Deloria, Jr. Copyright © 1970 by Vine Deloria, Jr.

Reprinted from *God Is Red* by Vine Deloria, Jr., with permission of the author.

Reprinted from *The Metaphysics of Modern Existence* by Vine Deloria, Jr., with permission of the author.

From *Dharma and Development: Religion as Resource in the Sarvodaya Self-Help Movement* by Joanna Macy (West Hartford, Conn.: Kumarian Press, Inc., 14 Oakwood Avenue, West Hartford, CT 06119 USA, 1985).

Reprinted without changes from *Mutual Causality in Buddhism and General Systems Theory* by Joanna Macy, by permission of the State University of New York Press. © 1991, State University of New York. All rights reserved.

Reprinted from *World As Lover, World As Self* (1991) by Joanna Macy with permission of Parallax Press, Berkeley, California.

From *Gitanjali* by Rabindranath Tagore (New York: Scribner, 1997).

From *The Religion of Man* by Rabindranath Tagore by permission of HarperCollins Publishers Ltd.

Reprinted from *A Tagore Reader,* edited by Amiya Chakravarty, with permission of Visva-Bharati University, Calcutta, India.

From *Dorothy Day: Selected Writings,* edited by Robert Ellsberg. Copyright © 1983, 1992 by Robert Ellsberg and Tamar Hennessey. Published in 1992 by Orbis Books, Maryknoll, N. Y. 10545.

Introduction

Where does the human longing for spiritual meaning come from? Why do people express this longing through religious devotion and participation in the world? What nurtures persons' growth in spiritual awareness? What prompts them to carry out acts of compassion and justice in response to the needs they perceive around them?

The answers to these questions are so complex—and yet so fascinating—that I felt compelled to set out on a journey of study and reflection. This book is the result of that journey. This is a book of stories: stories of people well known and not so well known, individuals who represent different cultures and religious faith traditions, persons who seek to combine spiritual nurture with acts of compassion and justice, spiritual seekers who are not so very different from us in their day-to-day quest for meaning in their lives. In hearing stories from their lives we get a sense of what spirituality is, what it looks like to live a spiritually energized life, and what nurtures that life in the Spirit.

What Is "Engaged Spirituality"?

The individuals whose life stories are told in this book are different from each other in many ways, but all of them share a characteristic that I call an "engaged spirituality." I borrow this term from one of the persons described in this book, Zen Buddhist monk Thich Nhat Hanh. He calls his own religious commitment "engaged Buddhism" to suggest the way that his study of classic Buddhist teachings empowers him to engage the world in creative, life-affirming ways. In a more general sense, engaged spirituality is demonstrated by all those persons who find within their faith tradition the resources that nurture their being and enable them to engage in activities that move the world toward peace, justice, greater compassion, and wholeness. At the same time, persons dedicated to an engaged spirituality find that their involvement in social causes and actions to transform the world inevitably leads them back to those nurturing resources. When viewed in this larger sense, engaged spirituality involves living a dual engagement: engaging with those resources that provide spiritual nurture *and* engaging with the world through acts of compassion and justice. Engaged spirituality is not an either/or prospect, but a conscious and intentional commitment to engage both the nurturing and the active aspects of religious faith.

Engaged spirituality challenges the notion that the spiritual life is made up only of quiet activities like prayer, contemplation, study, and private religious pursuits. The lives described here demonstrate that the spiritual life can also include the busy—often noisy—activities of protest, writing about and speaking out against injustice, and offering compassionate and loving care to those in need. Indeed, these persons would say that the spiritual life *must* include all of these activities in order to be authentic, life-changing, and world-transforming. This book of life stories, readings, and action/reflection exercises provides a glimpse into how this holistic spirituality is actually practiced by people of faith. Not only can we learn what engaged spirituality looks like, but we can also discover how to capture the essence of this spiritual commitment for our own lives.

About the Format of the Book

Each chapter leads the reader(s) through four phases: Prepare to Meditate, Hear the Stories, Read the Words, and Reflect and Act. *Prepare to Meditate* is a centering exercise that sets the stage for the study and reflection that follow.

The main body of each chapter is entitled *Hear the Stories.* Because this is not a book of biographies, but rather a book of stories, we enter into the lives of each person by hearing formative stories from their lives. We experience with them the heights and the depths of daily life. We witness the joys and inevitable struggles of making a commitment to a life that combines spiritual nurture with acts of compassion and justice.

After hearing the stories, we can *Read the Words* that were written and spoken by each of the persons profiled. These words give us another way of seeing how that person expresses her or his spirituality in the midst of a world that often does not put much stock in things that cannot be adequately measured and explained.

Following the written words are several exercises that call us to *Reflect and Act.* They are intended to enable us to receive, in a more experiential way, the ideas expressed in the stories and readings. Even more, they challenge us to grow in awareness of engaged spirituality by leading us to expand beyond our comfortable boundaries. They call for silence, deep thinking, artistic expression, and intentional activity.

How to Use This Book

This study book is intended for use by individuals and groups. An individual might choose to spend one week studying and reflecting on each chapter. Begin each session with the centering exercise called *Prepare to Meditate.* Another meditative exercise could be substituted for the one presented at the beginning of the chapter. Then begin to engage the stories, readings, and exercises contained within the chapter. Here is a suggested schedule for the week:

Sunday:	*Hear the Stories*
	Engage one exercise of your choice from *Reflect and Act*
Monday:	Reading One from *Read the Words*
	Engage one exercise
Tuesday:	Reading Two
	Engage one exercise
Wednesday:	Reading Three
	Engage one exercise
Thursday:	Reading Four
	Engage one exercise
Friday:	Reading Five
	Engage one exercise
Saturday:	Review and journal-writing

Feel free to alter this schedule so that it meets your interests and needs. For additional inspiration, I encourage you to look at the resources under the heading *For Further Reading* listed at the conclusion of the chapter.

Small groups should plan to spend at least one hour studying each chapter. One member of the group could volunteer to lead the other members through the process of study and reflection. That same person might be invited to facilitate every meeting, or leadership could rotate among the members. The facilitator may begin by inviting everyone to participate in the centering exercise. Then the group can move together to the section entitled *Hear the Stories*. There are several ways the group might work their way through the life stories:

1. The members could be asked to read the stories ahead of time. At the time of the group meeting it would be helpful if one person would volunteer to recount the highlights of the chapter in order to refresh the memories of the other members and to provide a framework for those who did not have the opportunity to read the material.

2. Ask one or two members who are good public speakers to read the stories for the entire group. Ideally the readers should receive the text ahead of time so that they can adequately prepare. Since the stories are presented in narrative form, another possibility is to have members use drama or pantomime to communicate them to the others.

3. Provide silent time immediately following the centering exercise to allow individuals to read the stories on their own. If this option is chosen, please be sensitive to the fact that all people read and absorb material at a different rate. Be careful not to rush anyone who needs a few extra minutes to read the passage in silence. Invite those who finish quickly to use the time for additional reflection and personal preparation for the class. The leader might wish to provide paper and pencils or art materials so that the participants can respond to what they have read.

When all are ready, have the group reflect on the following three questions:

1. What part of the person's story do I identify with the most? Why?

2. How does this person's life exemplify the union of spiritual nurture and acts of compassion and justice?

3. How does this person's story challenge me and our faith community?

Using the same questions each week will give the group members a framework to guide their weekly reading.

Invite the group members to read aloud one or two selections from *Read the Words*. Divide into smaller groups of two or three people to engage in one of the reflection and action exercises. As much as possible, encourage the members to covenant with one another to carry out the intended action during the subsequent week. Additional reading and reflection could also be done using the suggestions in the *For Further Reading* section. Conclude the group time with words of encouragement and a prayer of blessing.

A Word about Inclusive Language

Many of the writings included in this collection were written before the time of heightened awareness about the importance of inclusive language. I believe that when the word "men" is used by these writers, most often they intend it to mean "men and women." Therefore, rather than tamper with the language, I have left the writings as they were originally penned. Our sensitive modern ears and eyes, however, are often disturbed by such exclusivity (as they should be!). To bridge this gap, I suggest that when you encounter those passages written with exclusively male language, read them twice, once with male pronouns and a second time with female pronouns. Not only will this exercise remind you that the writer intended to include both men and women in her or his statement, but it will also give you new eyes and ears for understanding those words.

Keeping a Journal

Other spiritual seekers who have graciously read these chapters have told me of the benefits they have received from keeping a journal while studying and contemplating these different lives. Journaling has the distinct advantage of allowing the reader to uncover deep meanings by entering into a dialogue with the life story and writings of each individual person profiled in this book. In the schedule I have offered above, I suggest that the reader use the last day of the week to journal and review the past week. A journaling component could very easily be included each day as well: Writing in a journal could follow the reading and action/reflection exercise, or, on certain days, journaling could replace the action/reflection exercise altogether. For those using this book in a small group, keeping individual journals would provide a sense of continuity across the week—or longer— between group meetings. During the course of the meeting, persons could be invited to share an insight from their journals. However, because a journal is the place where we set down our most intimate thoughts, no one should ever be coerced into sharing what has been written. For more information on maintaining a journal, please look at the books listed in the *For Further Reading* section.

FOR THE SPIRITUAL JOURNEY

There is an intense hunger for spirituality throughout our world. I feel it in my life; I observe it in the lives of others. The food to nourish our hungry spirits and the water to quench our thirsty souls is all around us. It is my hope that through this encounter with people who have been fed by Divine Spirit, we ourselves may welcome the Spirit into our lives and be empowered to act on God's behalf in our world.

A WORD OF THANKS

First, thank you to Mary Elizabeth Moore, the first person— other than myself—to get excited about this project. Her careful reading and ongoing enthusiasm gave me the energy to see this through to the end.

Thanks also to my editor, David Polk. He supported this book from the moment he heard about it and always believed it would be published.

Finally, thank you to the friends who read, meditated upon, and critically engaged the manuscript: Lois McAfee, Caroline Merrill, Don Stuart, Carol Trinca, and Glenn Watkins. Their participation made the book much better than I alone could have done.

For Further Reading

**Books on the union of spiritual nurture
and acts of compassion and justice**

Brown, Robert McAfee. *Spirituality and Liberation: Overcoming the Great Fallacy.* Louisville: Westminster Press, 1988.

Dorr, Donal. *Spirituality and Justice.* Maryknoll, N.Y.: Orbis Books, 1984.

Harris, Maria. *Proclaim Jubilee! A Spirituality for the Twenty-First Century.* Louisville: Westminster John Knox Press, 1996.

Nouwen, Henri. *Reaching Out: The Three Movements of the Spiritual Life.* New York: Doubleday Books, 1975.

Palmer, Parker J. *The Active Life.* San Francisco: Harper SanFrancisco, 1991.

Books on journaling

Broyles, Anne. *Journaling: A Spirit Journey.* Nashville: The Upper Room, 1988.

Kelsey, Morton T. *Adventure Inward: Christian Growth Through Personal Journal Writing.* Minneapolis: Augsburg Press, 1980.

Progoff, Ira. *At a Journal Workshop.* New York: Dialogue House, 1977.

Chapter One

Howard Thurman

Seeking Understanding among People of Different Faiths

PREPARE TO MEDITATE

Light a candle and sit quietly, away from distractions such as the television and telephone. Breathe in and breathe out, consciously feeling and hearing each breath. Concentrate on the phrase, "I am surrounded by the love of God." Breathe in "I am surrounded," breathe out "by the love of God." Do this slowly, but not uncomfortably so, for several minutes. When you are relaxed and open, move on to the stories or readings.

HEAR THE STORIES

Minister, teacher, writer, mystic—these and many other words have been used to describe the man Howard Thurman. He is best known for his thirst for knowledge, his hunger for God, and his incomparable efforts to bring these experiences into the lives of those around him. These stories from his life and writings from his pen continue to be an inspiration to all who seek to live the life of faith as he did.

Born in 1900, Thurman grew up in poverty in Daytona Beach, Florida. Due to his father's death when he was seven years old, he was raised by his mother and grandmother, women of devout faith. He was also nurtured and guided by the African American community of which he was part, most notably the Baptist church his family attended.

At the age of twelve Howard decided to join the church, as is the Baptist tradition. He went to the deacons of the church to announce his intention and be questioned by them. When young Howard told them he wanted to be a Christian, they turned him away, saying that he should return to them after he had been converted and could tell them without hesitation that he was already a Christian. The distraught preteen returned home and relayed the story to his grandmother. She immediately took him by the hand and walked him back to the church, where she confronted the deacons about their decision. "How dare you turn this boy down?" she demanded. "He is a Christian and was one long before he came to you today. Maybe you did not understand his word, but shame on you if you do not know his heart. Now you take this boy into the church right now—before you close this meeting!" And it was done.

The following Sunday Thurman was baptized in the Halifax River. Wearing white robes, the baptismal candidates formed a procession that wound its way from the church to the river. Behind them walked the church members and other witnesses. A gospel singer led the way, singing the verses of a hymn as the enthusiastic crowd of worshipers replied, "Let's go down to Jordan, Hallelujah!" Each candidate was led by two deacons, one who stood in the river to mark the spot where the baptism would take place, and a second man who led the candidate into the water. It was in this way that the minister baptized young Howard Thurman in the name of the Father, Son, and Holy Ghost.

What Thurman soon discovered was that his most rigorous religious training took place after his baptism. He was assigned two sponsors, a man and a woman, who met with him every Tuesday afternoon to instruct him in living the Christian life. He was taught how to lead hymn-singing, pray aloud in public, and officiate at a prayer meeting. His final test was to lead an adult prayer service. Having satisfactorily completed the process, Thurman was now a full member of the church. Through it all, his sponsors made clear to him that in becoming a Christian, he had taken on a new way of living. He also knew that he did not make this journey alone, for the members of his church and family stood nearby to support him in his new life.

His first great challenge came to him the day after his baptism. He was fishing out on the river when he was confronted by rain and a fierce wind. As he was trying to make his way through the storm, the oar slipped from his hands, and he fell backward in the boat, hitting his head on the wooden seat. He began to curse in anger, only to remember with shame that he had been baptized in these same waters just the day before. Young Howard cried all afternoon. With a contrite heart he confessed his transgression to his sponsor. In her wisdom, she not only consoled him but warned him to beware of the many temptations to turn away from God. In his autobiography Thurman writes: "Looking back, it is clear to me that the watchful attention of my sponsors in the church served to enhance my consciousness that whatever I did with my life *mattered*."[1]

The disciplines of prayer and service were incorporated into Thurman's life at a young age. He discovered that one of the best ways to enter into a spirit of prayer was through the practice of silence. He writes of one of his earliest experiences:

> As a child I was accustomed to spend many hours alone in my rowboat, fishing along the river, when there was no sound save the lapping of the waves against the boat. There were times when it seemed as if the earth and the river and the sky and I were one beat of the same pulse. It was a time of watching and waiting for what I did not know—yet I always knew. There would come a moment when beyond the single pulse beat there was a sense of Presence which seemed always to speak to me. My response to the sense of Presence always had the quality of personal communion. There was no voice. There was no image. There was no vision. There was God.[2]

Thurman's love of reading and learning led him to seek further education: attending a Baptist high school in Jacksonville, Florida, going to Morehouse College in Atlanta, Georgia, and studying for the ministry at Rochester Theological Seminary. His first pastorate was in Oberlin, Ohio. There he and his wife Kate gave birth to their daughter Olive. Sadly, Kate died of tuberculosis in 1930.

To further develop his interest in spirituality, Thurman pursued a Ph.D. by studying with the Quaker mystic Rufus Jones at Haverford College in Pennsylvania. He began his teaching career at Morehouse and Spelman Colleges in Atlanta. In 1932 he married Sue Bailey, and together they moved to Washington, D.C., where he taught classes in religion and later became the dean of the chapel at Howard University, the premier university for blacks in the nation's capital. It was during this time that their daughter Anne was born.

While at Howard, Thurman's excellent skills as a preacher, teacher, and spiritual leader developed more fully. The numbers of those who attended chapel services grew, and the membership knew no limitations according to sex, race, social status, or religious affiliation. He grew more and more in his conviction that spirituality has no boundaries. He came to believe "that the things that are true in any religious experience are to be found in that religious experience precisely because they are true; they are not true simply because they are found in that religious experience."[3] It was with this in mind that he accepted the invitation to go to India as an ambassador of goodwill.

While in India, Thurman and his wife traveled throughout the country meeting many devout Hindus. A highlight of their journey was a day spent with Gandhi, a man with whom Thurman felt a deep kinship. They also met Rabindranath Tagore, the Indian poet and mystic who, in his writings, sought to show the evils of social and political exclusivism.

Perhaps the most interesting encounter Thurman had while in India was with Dr. Singh, the professor who directed the program in oriental studies at Tagore's university, Shantiniketan. All morning the two of them talked about the beliefs, practices, and history of the three religious traditions they knew best: Buddhism, Hinduism, and Christianity. Thurman had a lunch engagement so, at the appointed time, he stood to excuse himself to go to meet his hosts. As he did so, Singh noticed that Thurman was quietly laughing. Of course, Thurman noticed that Singh, too, was chuckling to himself.

When Singh asked Thurman to explain the cause of his amusement, Thurman observed that these two learned men had spent their entire morning acting as if they were engaged in battle. Singh, a Hindu, and Thurman, a Christian, had sparred for position, each extolling the virtues of his own tradition while gently attacking the other. "You are right," said Singh. "When we come back this afternoon, let us be wiser than that."

That afternoon they did return to their conversation, but did so with a new intention and point of view. Thurman writes,

> It was as if we had stepped out of social, political, cultural frames of reference, and allowed two human spirits to unite on a ground of reality that was unmarked by separateness and differences. This was a watershed of experience in my life. We had become a part of each other even as we remained essentially individual. I was able to stand secure in my place and enter into his place without diminishing myself or threatening him.[4]

Through this experience and others like it in India, Thurman became convinced of the need for a worshiping community that would embrace all people, despite gender, race, social status, or religious affiliation. Upon his return to Howard University, he became much more intentional about developing worship and educational experiences that drew people in from all sectors of society.

The culmination of this dream of inclusivity came in 1944 when he accepted the invitation to go to San Francisco to become the co-pastor of the newly formed Church for the Fellowship of All Peoples. This interracial, all-inclusive ministry was indeed experimental; nothing like this had ever been attempted before. Through the use of creative music and dance, through education and the cultivation of the Spirit in silence, and through fellowship events and uplifting worship services, Thurman brought people together around common interests and concerns.

After nine years at Fellowship Church, Thurman was called to Boston to be the dean of Marsh Chapel at Boston University. This was another first for the influential and well-respected preacher and teacher; it was highly unusual and somewhat controversial that a black man serve as the dean of the chapel at a major university. Nevertheless, he and his wife, Sue, were thrilled to have the opportunity to work again with college students. Through worship services, study classes, and fellowship opportunities, they sought to duplicate, as much as possible, the inclusive ministry they had developed while in San Francisco.

The following story from his days at Marsh Chapel illustrates the immense impact Thurman's ministry had on those who experienced it. A young Japanese woman committed suicide. She was a graduate student who also worked as a night nurse at a local hospital. She killed herself after viewing a movie that showed the Japanese people in an extremely unfavorable light. She left a note that read, "Even here I have no friends."

Thurman was asked to arrange for her funeral, since she had no family in the United States. The day before the service, however, her two sisters arrived from Japan. Talking with them about their sister and the service he was to conduct, he could not help but feel empty inside. "It was one of the most desolate moments that I ever experienced in all my ministry," he said later, "because I felt we had failed both the dead girl and now her two sisters, who were in Boston among strangers, a continent away from home."

The service was attended by the sisters and some doctors and nurses who worked at the hospital. The two women cried over their beloved sister and kissed her good-bye. Thurman accompanied the women and the casket to a waiting hearse. The young woman's body was to be taken back to Japan for burial.

What Thurman did not notice at the time was that the university's groundskeepers and custodians had gathered outside the chapel, watching the funeral procession. Word of the woman's death had spread throughout the university community. All were wondering how Dean Thurman would handle this funeral. It was a funeral many other pastors would eagerly avoid: she had committed suicide, she was Japanese, and she did not attend chapel services. Despite these things, Thurman gladly ministered to her family, friends, and co-workers. From that point on, Thurman says, members of the university community looked upon him in a different way because they perceived, in the way he handled a difficult funeral, the real mission and meaning of his work at the chapel.[5]

Howard and Sue Thurman retired to San Francisco in 1965. From then until his death in 1981, he spent his time writing, lecturing, and preaching. You are invited to read the portions of his prose and poetry that follow this section. Throughout his life he sought to draw closer to God, through prayer, silence, encounters with the natural world, communion with others, and acts of service. His was a life of faith and action.

READ THE WORDS

As you read the works that follow, ask yourself these questions: What are some ways in which Thurman's writings connect to his life story? How do these words nurture my spiritual life and/or inspire me to engage in acts of social justice?

READING ONE:

In Disciplines of the Spirit, *Thurman reflects on the various spiritual disciplines in which he feels that we as religious people should participate. The following are words about the meaning of commitment.*

The meaning of commitment as a discipline of the spirit must take into account that mind and spirit cannot be separated from the body in any absolute sense. It has been wisely said that the time and the place of man's life on earth is the time and the place of his body, but the meaning of his life is as significant and eternal as he wills to make it. While he is on earth, his mind and spirit are domiciled in his body, bound up in a creature who is at once a child of nature and of God. Commitment means that it is possible for a man to yield the nerve center of his consent to a purpose or cause, a movement or an ideal, which may be more important to him than whether he lives or dies. The commitment is a self-conscious act of will by which he affirms his identification with what he is committed to. The character of his commitment is determined by that to which the center or core of his consent is given.[6]

READING TWO:

Deep Is the Hunger *and* Meditations of the Heart *are both collections of short meditative pieces that Thurman wrote for use at The Church for the Fellowship of All Peoples. In the following story, contained in* Deep Is the Hunger, *Thurman guides the reader in expanding the notion of spirituality and social responsibility beyond the confines of human relationships.*

It was just an ordinary dog in distress. My friend had never seen him before. Twenty minutes previously he did not know that the animal existed. Suddenly, he saw him struggling in shallow water, his body covered with a thick coat of crude oil. My friend stopped his car, jumped out, called to the dog but soon discovered that he was too exhausted to make the shore. Without a moment's hesitation, he went down into the water above his knees and so to the rescue. At first, the dog tried to get away, thinking that here was another enemy, or the same one who had thrown him in. At last, it was clear to the frightened animal that here was salvation. A complete change came over his entire body; he relaxed, even as an automatic shiver passed over him, again and again. Together, dog and man, wet, oily and somewhat bedraggled, made their way to the nearest veterinarian. Arrangements were completed for the dog to be washed, treated and fed. Very often, we are reminded of the story of the Good Samaritan. We apply it almost instantly to stark human need when we are brought face to face with it. To apply it to so-called dumb animals requires an extra something, an added ingredient of sensitiveness. To meet human need, after all, may be regarded as an act of self-defense or the working out from under a bad conscience. To meet the need of an animal for which one has not developed any affection is a mark of graciousness of spirit devoutly to be wished. As I reflect upon the meaning of this simple act as a revelation of the authentic character of my friend, I am moved to voice a simple thanksgiving to God that I know such a man. Are you such a person? Am I?[7]

READING THREE:

Thurman often wrote poetry as a way of expressing his deepest spiritual and social passions. This prayer from Meditations of the Heart *is illustrative of the concerns that touched him most profoundly.*

I CONFESS

The concern which I lay bare before God today is:

My concern for the life of the world
    in these troubled times.
I confess my own inner confusion
    as I look out upon the world.

There is food for all—many are hungry.
There are clothes enough for all—many are in rags.
There is room enough for all—many are crowded.
There are none who want war—preparations for
    conflict abound.

I confess my own share in the ills of the times.
    I have shirked my own responsibilities as a citizen.
    I have not been wise in casting my ballot.
    I have left to others a real interest in making a
        public opinion worthy of democracy.
    I have been concerned about my own little job,
        my own little security, my own shelter,
        my own bread.

I have not really cared about jobs for others,
    security for others, shelter for others,
        bread for others.
    I have not worked for peace; I want peace,
        but I have voted and worked for war.
    I have silenced my own voice that it may not be
        heard on the side of any cause, however right,
        if it meant running risks or damaging my own
        little reputation.

Let Thy light burn in me that I may, from this moment
    on, take effective steps within my own powers, to
    live up to the light and courageously to pray for the
    kind of world I so deeply desire.[8]

READING FOUR:

The experience of discrimination in American society informed much of what Thurman believed about the need for love and acceptance among all peoples. In this piece from Jesus and the Disinherited, *he calls for those who profess Christ to overcome the separations that cause all people to suffer.*

It is necessary, therefore, for the privileged and the under-privileged to work on the common environment for the purpose of providing normal experiences of fellowship. This is one very important reason for the insistence that segregation is a complete ethical and moral evil. Whatever it may do for those who dwell on either side of the wall, one thing is certain: it poisons all normal contacts of those persons involved. The first step toward love is a common sharing of a sense of mutual worth and value...

The experience of the common worship of God is such a moment. It is in this connection that American Christianity has betrayed the religion of Jesus almost beyond redemption. Churches have been established for the underprivileged, for the weak, for the poor, on the theory that they prefer to be among themselves. Churches have been established for the Chinese, the Japanese, the Korean, the Mexican, the Filipino, the Italian, and the Negro, with the same theory in mind. The result is that in the one place in which normal, free contacts might be most naturally established—in which the relations of the individual to his God should take priority over conditions of class, race, power, status, wealth, or the like—this place is one of the chief instruments for guaranteeing barriers.[9]

READING FIVE:

Thurman had a special love for nature and for all people. This prayer from Meditations of the Heart *helps us focus on both the joy and pain of living in our wonderful world.*

I am surrounded by the love of God.

The earth beneath my feet is the great womb out of which the life upon which my body depends comes in utter abundance. There is at work in the soil a mystery by which the death of one seed is transformed a thousandfold in newness of life. The magic wind, sun, and rain create a climate that nourishes every living thing. It is a law, and more than law; it is order, and more than order—there is a brooding tenderness out of which it all comes. In the contemplation of the earth, I know that I am surrounded by the love of God.

The events of my days strike a full balance of what seems both good and bad. Whatever may be the tensions and the stresses of a particular day, there is always lurking close at hand the trailing beauty of forgotten joy or unremembered peace. The weakness that engulfs me in its writhing toils reveals hidden strengths that could not show their face until my own desperation called them forth. In contemplation of the events of my days, I know that I am surrounded by the love of God.

The edge of hope that constantly invades the seasoned grounds of despair, the faith that keeps watch at the doors through which pass all the labors of my life and heart for what is right and true, the impulse to forgive and to seek forgiveness even when the injury is sharp and clear—these and countless other things make me know that by day and by night my life is surrounded by the love of God.

I am surrounded by the love of God.[10]

REFLECT AND ACT

By yourself, or in cooperation with others, engage in the following reflection and action exercises. Try to do one exercise each day for a week. If one activity is particularly meaningful, stay with it for a longer period of time. Also feel free to create exercises of your own as you are inspired by the life and witness of Howard Thurman.

1. Think back to your childhood and adolescence, and recall those people who were influential in teaching you and giving positive direction to your life. Were they parents, grandparents, a coach, a teacher, a pastor, a neighbor, or a community leader? Choose one person. Meditate on that person's influence in your younger life, and consider how that impact is still felt today. What is one thing you can do to express your appreciation to them this week?

2. Recall a time when you sensed the presence of God as Thurman did when he was sitting in the rowboat. Close your eyes and allow yourself to be transported to that place. What do you see, hear, smell, taste, and touch? Recreate the experience to the best of your abilities. Reflect on the circumstances that made that time a spiritual-filled moment. How can you create a climate in which such experiences of presence can happen more often?

3. Consider entering into a big brother or big sister relationship with a college student, teenager, or neighbor. Can this be done without resorting to condescension? How can mutuality, partnership, and cooperation be maximized?

4. Seek out and attend a worship service that is markedly different from your own. Reflect on the similarities and differences. How did this encounter with another religious tradition enhance or detract from your experience of worship?

5. Meditate on the words of Thurman's prayer "I Confess." Write your own prayer of confession, encompassing personal, interpersonal, and community transgressions. How will you make amends for the wrongs in which you have participated? Allow the assurance of divine forgiveness to fill you with peace.

6. Make a list of those people who live on the fringes of society. From that list choose one group of people who are marginalized. Do some research on this topic by going to the library, reading the newspaper, or interviewing members of this group. Answer the questions: Why are they marginalized? What are the economic, social, racial, and psychological factors that keep them there? What is one thing you can do to help improve life for people on the fringes?

7. Set aside ten minutes each day for silence. Open your mind, heart, and soul to hear the voice of God. If outside thoughts intrude, gently set them aside for later. Create an atmosphere in which the divine spirit can commune with your spirit.

8. Participate in some artistic endeavor: sing a song, play an instrument, write a poem, dance, paint, or draw. How does this activity speak to your soul?

9. With one or more people discuss those things that separate people from one another in one part of our world. Examine social, political, religious, economic, and psychological dimensions. What is something you can do to facilitate communication among those who are different from one another?

10. Reflect on Thurman's words about nature. Consider the ways in which humanity uses and abuses the world's natural resources. What is an appropriate human response to nature? Determine one thing you will do this week to express your appreciation and care for God's creation.

For Further Reading

Thurman, Anne Spencer, ed. *For the Inward Journey: The Writings of Howard Thurman.* New York: Harcourt Brace Jovanovich, 1984.

Thurman, Howard. *Jesus and the Disinherited.* Nashville: Abingdon Press, 1949.

——. *Deep Is the Hunger.* New York: Harper and Brothers, 1951.

——. *Meditations of the Heart.* New York: Harper and Row, 1953.

——. *Disciplines of the Spirit.* New York: Harper and Row, 1963.

——.*The Centering Moment.* Richmond, Ind.: Friends United Press, 1969.

——.*With Head and Heart.* New York: Harcourt Brace Jovanovich, 1979.

Notes

[1] Howard Thurman, *With Head and Heart* (New York: Harcourt Brace Jovanovich, 1979), 18–20.

[2] Howard Thurman, *Disciplines of the Spirit* (New York: Harper and Row, 1963), 96.

[3] Thurman, *With Head and Heart,* 120.

[4] Ibid., 129.

[5] Ibid., 183–85.

[6] Thurman, *Disciplines of the Spirit,* 17.

[7] Howard Thurman, *Deep Is the Hunger* (New York: Harper and Brothers, 1951), 86–87.

[8] Howard Thurman, *Meditations of the Heart* (New York: Harper and Row, 1953), 195–96.

[9] Howard Thurman, *Jesus and the Disinherited* (Nashville: Abingdon Press, 1949), 98.

[10] Thurman, *Meditations of the Heart,* 210–12.

Chapter Two

Simone Weil

To Live and Work
as One of the Simple Folk

PREPARE TO MEDITATE

Light a candle, sit quietly, and allow your body to relax. Think back to a time you felt compelled to identify with someone who was suffering. Recreate the circumstances in your mind, being attuned to the thoughts, emotions, and bodily sensations the situation created within you.

HEAR THE STORIES

Simone Weil was born in Paris in 1909. Her father was a doctor and theirs was a middle-class family. Consequently, the family traveled widely, and the Weil children were provided with a fine education. Her brother was a mathematical genius and, though she was also quite intelligent, Weil often felt inferior to him. Hers was a nominally Jewish family, and she received no religious upbringing whatsoever.

Paris was a city of luxury at the turn of the century. At the same time, however, it was a divided city. Many sharp social divisions had existed since the French Revolution: Black and Red, Right and Left, rich and poor. Few people sought to cross those boundaries. Simone Weil was one person who did. Her first leanings toward social action were displayed during the First World War. She refused to eat sugar throughout the war years because the soldiers on the front did not have it to eat. Likewise, she would not wear socks when she was a little girl, because she knew that poor children did not have them to wear.

As a young woman, she placed first in the nationwide competition for the *École Normale Supérieure*, a teaching college recently opened to women. She graduated with highest honors and became a teacher. Even more, she went beyond her educational pursuits to become actively involved in overcoming the political and social problems of her day.

Her first teaching assignment was in Le Puy where she taught philosophy to young women preparing to go to the university. Although brilliant, she was not especially accessible to her students: she spoke in a monotone voice, rarely looked up from her lecture notes, dressed noticeably poorly, was clumsy and eccentric, and was a chain-smoker who had an incessant cough. On the positive side, she treated her students as equal colleagues and sought to help them grow in their love of knowledge rather than merely prepare for college entrance exams.

It was during her time at Le Puy that she first became involved in political activism. She was a member of the middle class and, as such, many believed that she had no reason to show interest in the plight of the poor. Despite this, she felt the need to identify with the poor in their suffering and did this by living in a small room in a poor neighborhood, with no heat and little food. What money she did have she donated to workers' causes.

At one point during her time at Le Puy, a group of unemployed workers sought an audience with the mayor of the city. Weil volunteered to head their delegation. Articles in the local newspaper questioned her motives for such activity, citing her excellent pay as a professor as proof that she obviously couldn't have pure motives for being concerned with the working people. As a result, she was investigated by the police, and a report was given to her superiors in the school system, seriously endangering her teaching position. Weil could not be intimidated so easily. She continued to consort with workers in the cafes and took part in subsequent demonstrations. She also conspicuously displayed a copy of a communist newspaper whenever she ventured out into the city of Le Puy.

The government of Le Puy responded by banning all demonstrations and processions. Weil then led the unemployed workers in small groups to the labor exchange office where they continued to make their presence known. One day police officers met the workers as they left the building in order to search and question them about their activities. In response, the workers formed a procession and marched through the streets of the city singing. At the front of the line was Simone Weil, carrying the red flag of the united workers.

Intense pressure was placed on the school at Le Puy to remove Weil and replace her with a less controversial teacher. Many of the parents felt she was a bad influence on their daughters. Her own students, however, had signed a petition declaring that their teacher was impartial and that they valued her teaching. Despite this, Weil was forced to sign a letter of transfer. In the next academic year, she took up a new teaching post in another town.[1]

Although she was influenced by Marxist thought, Weil never became a communist. She soon found Marxism inadequate to explain the situation of the workers. She saw that the workers provided the most important element in the industrialization process—the work of their own hands. She believed it was essential for the workers to understand how the work that they do fits into the entire production process, and that they should not be forced merely to recreate the same act over and over again in some meaningless way. Even more, she called for a realignment of the power structure so that the workers could have more personal control and pride in their work.

After three years of teaching she determined that it was best to take a leave of absence in order to work in a factory. She began by working with heavy machinery. However, she lacked the physical strength for such work and was so plagued by headaches that she soon moved on to work as a packer in a small shop. Finally, she worked on an assembly line in a car factory. After several months she had to leave this work for fear that it would destroy her physically. In reflecting on this time she writes:

> What I went through there marked me in so lasting a
> manner that still today when any human being, who-
> ever he may be and in whatever circumstances, speaks
> to me without brutality, I cannot help having the

> impression that there must be some mistake and that
> unfortunately the mistake will in all probability disap-
> pear. There I received forever the mark of a slave, like
> the branding of the red-hot iron the Romans put on the
> foreheads of their most despised slaves. Since then I have
> always regarded myself as a slave.[2]

As a result of her time in the factory, she felt that her body and soul had been destroyed. She was well aware of physical afflic-tion, since she had suffered from headaches most of her life. But this was an affliction of a different sort, one that took in the suffering of all the people who were dehumanized by the mean-ingless factory work in which they engaged.

Her parents took her to Portugal to recuperate before she returned to teaching. She tells of her first religious experience, which occurred while she traveled alone in a Portuguese fishing village. As she made her way through the fishing village, she realized that the people there looked just as awful and sad as she felt. That night the villagers celebrated the festival of their patron saint. The women walked in solemn procession under the light of the full moon. They carried candles and sang songs that sounded like funeral dirges as they made the rounds from boat to boat. Weil was deeply moved by the devotion of these simple people. Within her arose the conviction that Christianity is the religion of slaves and that, as a slave herself, she could not help but belong to it.[3]

Weil had returned to teaching for only two years when she felt compelled to participate in the Spanish Civil War in 1936. This war caught the interest of many intellectuals in Britain, France, and the United States who understood it as a clear con-flict between militant fascism and revolutionary freedom. While she was there she insisted on going to the front line to be among her working comrades. Assigned to be a cook, she spilled boil-ing water on her leg and had to go to the hospital. Interestingly enough, Weil discovered that she learned more about war by visiting the wounded in the hospital than she had by being on the front line. After just two months in Spain, she came back to France, disillusioned and depressed.[4]

From 1937 on, Weil's health deteriorated so greatly that she could not teach regularly. Thus it was that her life took a decided turn toward the religious dimension. This emphasis on the religious life was not in contrast to the social dimension, but in conjunction with it. Her chief aim became discovering the will of God. Two pivotal experiences occurred during that next year. First, on a visit to Assisi in Italy she entered a twelfth-century chapel where Saint Francis himself had often come to pray. For the first time in her life she was compelled to fall on her knees in devotion to God. The second crucial experience was on Palm Sunday at Solesmes Monastery, where the Benedictine monks sang Gregorian chants. As she continued to suffer from severe headaches, each sound from the mouths of the monks was like a blow to the head. She found, however, that by concentrating on the beauty of the chants she was able to rise above the pain. For the first time in her life, she felt a oneness with the passion of Christ.[5]

Weil's biographer explains the relationship between her social action and her spiritual life:

> The willing acceptance of the pains of the flesh and of the harsh, cold, brutal "necessity" of the world was for Simone Weil one of the chief ways to the silent presence of the divine reality. But her mysticism was never a flight from reality here below into a wholly other reality above…redemption consisted precisely in the harmonization of contraries, in the attainment to that state of the soul in which suffering and glory become one…And the point at which those intensities met was the cross of Christ.[6]

Weil was introduced to the poetry of the seventeenth century English poet George Herbert. His poems on religious themes have been read devotionally for several hundred years. Weil was especially touched by his poem called "Love," which tells of God's pursuit of one soul who deemed himself unworthy of Love's attentions. She often recited this poem in its entirety, almost as if it were a prayer. She memorized it and found that if she said the words during the worst moments of a violent headache, she could work through the unbearable pain. During one such recitation, she says, "Christ himself came down and took possession of me."[7]

With the beginning of the Second World War, Weil sought out the opportunity to work with the French Resistance. Although she wanted to go behind enemy lines, her poor health allowed her only to do intellectual writings on behalf of the French Resistance. She continued her practice of refusing to eat any more than the most meager food rations. At times she ate even less, thinking that what she didn't eat would feed the troops fighting the war. Weil died in August 1943 at the age of thirty-four. The cause of death was listed as self-starvation and tuberculosis. Even at the end of her life, she was committed to identifying with the working men and women, to live and work as they did.

READ THE WORDS

As you read the works that follow, ask yourself these questions: What are some ways in which Weil's writings connect to her life story? How do these words nurture your spiritual life and/or inspire you to engage in acts of social justice?

READING ONE:

Weil kept a journal during the time that she worked in the factories engaging in monotonous, physically exhausting work. She chronicles her relationships with her coworkers, the humiliation heaped on her by supervisors, and the physical and emotional toll this work had on her. This is the final entry from Weil's Factory Journal, *1934:*

Gained from this experience? The feeling that I do not possess any right whatever, of any kind (take care not to lose this feeling). The ability to be morally self-sufficient, to live in this state of constant latent humiliation without feeling humiliated in my own eyes; to savor intensely every moment of freedom or camaraderie, as if it would last forever. A direct contact with life.

I came near to being broken. I almost was—my courage, the feeling that I had value as a person were nearly broken during a period I would be humiliated to remember, were it not that strictly speaking I have retained no memory of it. I got up in the mornings with anguish. I went to the factory with dread; I worked like a slave; the noon break was a wrenching experience; I got back to my place at 5:45, preoccupied immediately with getting enough sleep (which I didn't) and with waking up early enough. Time was an intolerable burden. Dread—outright fear—of what was going to happen next only relaxed its grip on me on Saturday afternoon and Sunday morning. And what I dreaded was the *orders*.

The feeling of self-respect, such as it has been built up by society, is *destroyed*. It is necessary to forge another one for oneself (although exhaustion wipes out consciousness of one's ability to think!). Try to hold on to this other kind.

One finally gets a clear idea of one's own importance.

The class of those who *do not count*—in any situation—in anyone's eyes—and who will not count, ever, no matter what happens.[8]

READING TWO:

Gravity and Grace *is a compilation of Weil's musings on various topics, collected from the diaries she kept throughout her life. Here is profound reflection on the love of God.*

God's love for us is not the reason for which we should love him. God's love for us is the reason for us to love ourselves. How could we love ourselves without this motive?

It is impossible for man to love himself except in this roundabout way.[9]

READING THREE:

Weil's mystical experiences often occurred through the recitation of passages from great literature, something for which she had a deep love. In this following snippet from her book of religious reflections, Waiting for God, *we catch a glimpse of how this occurred for her when she recited the Lord's Prayer in Greek.*

Last summer, doing Greek with T_____, I went through the Our Father word for word in Greek. We promised each other to learn it by heart. I do not think he ever did so, but some weeks later, as I was turning over the pages of the Gospel, I said to myself that since I had promised to do this thing and it was good, I ought to do it. I did it. The infinite sweetness of this Greek text so took hold of me that for several days I could not stop myself from saying it over all the time. A week afterward I began the vine harvest. I recited the Our Father in Greek every day before work, and I repeated it very often in the vineyard.

Since that time I have made a practice of saying it through once each morning with absolute attention. If during the recitation my attention wanders or goes to sleep, in the minutest degree, I begin again until I have once succeeded in going through it with absolutely pure attention. Sometimes it comes about that I say it again out of sheer pleasure, but I only do it if I really feel the impulse.

The effect of this practice is extraordinary and surprises me every time, for, although I experience it each day, it exceeds my expectation at each repetition.

At times the very first words tear my thoughts from my body and transport it to a place outside space where there is neither perspective nor point of view. The infinity of the ordinary expanses of perception is replaced by an infinity to the second or sometimes the third degree. At the same time, filling every part of this infinity of infinity, there is silence, a silence which is not an absence of sound but which is the object of a positive sensation, more positive than that of sound. Noises, if there are any, only reach me after crossing this silence.

Sometimes, also, during this recitation or at other moments, Christ is present with me in person, but his presence is infinitely more real, more moving, more clear than on that first occasion when he took possession of me.[10]

READING FOUR:

Waiting for God *is a collection of Weil's religious writings from the last several years of her life. The book was assembled by her friend and confidante Father Perrin. In this excerpt, Weil talks of the powerful psychological relationship between joy and suffering, two emotions of which she was aware in a most intimate manner.*

Joy and suffering are two equally precious gifts both of which must be savored to the full, each one in its purity, without trying to mix them. Through joy, the beauty of the world penetrates our soul. Through suffering it penetrates our body. We could no more become friends of God through joy alone than one becomes a ship's captain by studying books of navigation. The body plays a part in all apprenticeships. On the place of physical sensibility, suffering alone gives us contact with that necessity which constitutes the order of the world, for pleasure does not involve an impression of necessity. It is a higher kind of sensibility, capable of recognizing a necessity of joy, and that only indirectly through a sense of beauty. In order that our being should one day become wholly sensitive in every part to this obedience that is the substance of matter, in order that a new sense should be formed in us to enable us to hear the universe as the vibration of the word of God, the transforming power of suffering and of joy are equally indispensable. When either of them comes to us we have to open the very center of our soul to it, just as a woman opens her door to messengers from her loved one. What does it matter to a lover if the messenger be polite or rough, so long as he delivers the message?[11]

READING FIVE:

What does it mean to have a calling to suffer? Weil reflects on this difficult question in another excerpt from Waiting for God.

The notion of vocation was like this for me. I saw that the carrying out of a vocation differed from the actions dictated by reason or inclination in that it was due to an impulse of an essentially and manifestly different order; and not to follow such an impulse when it made itself felt, even if it demanded impossibilities, seemed to me the greatest of all ills. Hence my conception of obedience; and I put this conception to the test when I entered the factory and stayed on there, even when I was in that state of intense and uninterrupted misery about which I recently told you. The most beautiful life possible has always seemed to me to be one where everything is determined, either by pressure of circumstances or by impulses such as I have just mentioned and where there is never any room for choice.[12]

READING SIX:

In this final excerpt from Waiting for God, *Weil muses on the challenge of loving others. She calls us to love, not out of pity but out of a sense of shared humanity.*

The love of our neighbor in all its fullness simply means being able to say to him: "What are you going through?" It is a recognition that the sufferer exists, not only as a unity in a collection, or a specimen from the social category labeled "unfortunate," but as a man, exactly like us, who was one day stamped with a special mark of affliction. For this reason it is enough, but it is indispensable, to know how to look at him in a certain way.

This way of looking is first of all attentive. The soul empties itself of all its own contents in order to receive into itself the being it is looking at, just as he is, in all his truth.

Only he who is capable of attention can do this.[13]

Reflect and Act

By yourself, or in cooperation with others, engage in the following reflection and action exercises. Try to do one exercise each day for a week. If one activity is particularly meaningful, stay with it for a longer period of time. Also feel free to create exercises of your own as you are inspired by the life and witness of Simone Weil.

1. Think back to a time when you worked hard physically. How did you feel about it at the time? Was it a good or bad experience for you? What made it that way? Did it have a spiritual dimension to it? Why or why not?

2. Spend several days reading the newspaper looking for signs of affliction in your neighborhood, nation, and world. Also look for signs of healing and hope. Besides expressing a willingness to pray for healing, are there other ways you might be willing to work to bring about social transformation? Commit to engage in one concrete action during this next week.

3. Meditate on God's love for you and for all of creation. Allow yourself to understand deeply the meaning of Weil's words: "God's love for us is the reason for us to love ourselves."

4. Simone Weil was so moved by "The Lord's Prayer" that she would often recite it in Greek. In addition, she wrote a line-by-line interpretation of the prayer.[14] Pray the prayer slowly, pausing to meditate on each phrase for a minute or two.

5. Reflect on your experiences with the mind-body-spirit connection. In what ways does affliction of the mind affect you physically and spiritually? How does physical affliction affect the mind and spirit? How is spiritual affliction manifest in the body and mind?

6. Recall an experience in which suffering and joy were powerfully intermingled. What confusion did this create for you? What deeper level of understanding did you reach?

7. Choose words to a poem, the words to a hymn, or the lyrics of a song that are especially meaningful to you. Read the words through once aloud. The second time through, read each line aloud, savoring the images the words create for you. If a particular thought is especially meaningful, hold on to it for a longer time. Allow the words to flow in and through you.

8. What does it mean to be obedient to the will of God? How are your present actions and beliefs affected by your sense of obedience? Ponder Weil's words on this subject: "The most beautiful life possible has always seemed to me to be one where everything is determined...and where there is never any room for choice."

9. Weil writes of the spiritual importance of being attentive to the needs of our neighbors. Who are your "neighbors"? Choose one person with whom you would not usually associate. What do you think are her concerns and struggles? What are his joys and hopes? Try to get beyond surface understanding and attempt to truly empathize with that other person at the very deepest level.

10. Keep a journal for a week. Take ten to fifteen minutes each day to write about and reflect on the events of the day. Be alert to the ways in which God's Spirit is active in your life and in the activities around you. If you find this exercise particularly meaningful, consider adopting journal writing as a regular spiritual discipline.

FOR FURTHER READING

Anderson, David. *Simone Weil.* London: SCM Press, 1971.

Davy, Marie-Magdeleine. *The Mysticism of Simone Weil.* Translated by Cynthia Rowland. Boston: Beacon Press, 1951.

Herbert, George. *The Poems of George Herbert.* London: Oxford University Press, 1961.

Weil, Simone. *Waiting for God.* Translated by Emma Craufurd. New York: G. P. Putnam's Sons, 1951.

——. *Gravity and Grace.* New York: G. P. Putnam's Sons, 1952.

——. *Formative Writings 1929–1941.* Translated and edited by Dorothy Tuck McFarland and Wilhelmina van Ness. Amherst: University of Massachusetts Press, 1987.

Notes

[1] David Anderson, *Simone Weil* (London: SCM, 1971), 29–31.

[2] Simone Weil, *Waiting for God,* trans. Emma Craufurd (New York: G. P. Putnam's Sons, 1951), 67.

[3] Ibid., 66–67.

[4] Anderson, 51.

[5] Weil, *Waiting for God,* 67–68.

[6] Anderson, 14–15.

[7] Weil, *Waiting for God,* 68–69.

[8] Simone Weil, *Formative Writings 1929–1941,* trans. and ed. Dorothy Tuck McFarland and Wilhelmina van Ness (Amherst: University of Massachusetts Press, 1987), 225.

[9] Simone Weil, *Gravity and Grace* (New York: G. P. Putnam's Sons, 1952), 111.

[10] Weil, *Waiting for God,* 71–72.

[11] Ibid., 132.

[12] Ibid., 63.

[13] Ibid., 115.

[14] See *Waiting for God,* 216–27.

Chapter Three

Elie Wiesel

That No One Should Ever Forget

PREPARE TO MEDITATE

In silence, recall a time of immense loss. This can be an event from your life, from the life of another, or from the life of the world. Be aware of the emotions this remembrance brings forth in you. Be aware of God's presence in the midst of this remembrance.

HEAR THE STORIES

The story is told of Rabbi Israel Baal Shem Tov who, when the Jewish people were threatened, would go to a special location in the forest to light a fire and say prayers. As a result, a miracle would happen, and the people would be spared from danger. Later on, a student of the rabbi found that he also had to intercede on behalf of the Jews. He went to the sacred place in the forest and offered a prayer to God, but he did not know how to light the fire. Again, the danger was prevented. Still later, a third rabbi went to the forest to ask God for a miracle for his people. This time, however, he did not know how to light the fire and he did not know what prayer to offer. Despite this, God looked upon the Jews with favor and gave them the miracle that preserved them. Finally, another misfortune compelled a fourth rabbi to seek the miracle. He sat in his chair and prayed, "I do not know how to light the fire. I do not know the words of the prayer. I do not even know where the sacred place in the forest

34

is located. All I can do is tell the story, and it must be enough."
And, so the legend goes, it *was* enough, and the crisis was
averted.[1]

This Hasidic tale is a fitting beginning to this chapter about
the life story of Elie Wiesel, a man who could be described as a
scholar and theologian, but who prefers to be known as a storyteller. As a survivor of the Holocaust, he sees himself as called
to be a messenger, to be the one who tells the story in such a
way that it can never be forgotten, so that the awful events can
never be repeated again. He has told the story many times in
many different ways: through his autobiographical novel, *Night*,
through fictionalized accounts of Holocaust survivors, and
through essays, dramas, and lectures.

Elie Wiesel's own story began in 1928, when he was born
in the small town of Sighet. Originally located in Hungary, Sighet
was part of Romania at the time of Wiesel's birth. Thus, he grew
up speaking both Hungarian and Romanian. He was the third of
four children and was the only son. Born into a devout Jewish
family, he attended a school where he studied scripture, Talmud, and complicated commentaries on the sacred texts. Wiesel's
father, Shlomo, was a merchant who owned a grocery store. His
mother Sarah was a learned and cultured woman. She dreamed
that one day her son, Eliezer, would be both a Ph.D. and a
rabbi.

Life changed dramatically for Wiesel and his family in 1944
when the Germans entered their country. All Jews were forced
into ghettoes. The family remained there for two weeks before
they were deported to the concentration camp. Wiesel and his
father were taken to the infamous camp Auschwitz/Birkenau,
and then to Buchenwald, where he remained until the camp
was liberated in 1945. Both of his parents and his youngest
sister were killed in the camps.

Ten years would pass before he would be able to confront
the anger and sense of betrayal he experienced as a result of the
Holocaust. His goal became to explore the ethical and theological implications of the silence of the world and the silence of a
God who allowed millions of European Jews and others to be
senselessly slaughtered under the Nazi regime. In his autobiographical novel he writes:

Never shall I forget that night, the first night in camp, which has turned my life into one long night, seven times cursed and seven times sealed. Never shall I forget that smoke.

Never shall I forget the little faces of the children, whose bodies I saw turned into wreathes of smoke beneath a silent blue sky.

Never shall I forget those flames which consumed my faith forever.

Never shall I forget that nocturnal silence which deprived me for all eternity of the desire to live. Never shall I forget those moments which murdered my God and my soul and turned my dreams into dust. Never shall I forget these things, even if I am condemned to live as long as God Himself. Never.[2]

After his liberation he moved to France where he studied literature, psychology, and philosophy at the Sorbonne. In Paris he worked as a correspondent for an Israeli newspaper. As the United Nations correspondent for the same paper, he was transferred to New York City in 1956. In 1963 he became a citizen of the United States. In the course of his work for the newspaper, he had occasion to travel to the Soviet Union twice. He also went to Israel numerous times and was there during the Six-Day War in 1967. In those places he saw firsthand the continued oppression of Jews, and he vowed to redouble his efforts to keep the memory of the Holocaust alive.

For this reason Wiesel decided to leave journalism in order to write novels, dramas, and essays full time. His writings chronicle his own journey from faith, to unfaith, and again to faith. The following story profiles his ambivalence and suggests a deeper spiritual life of which Wiesel himself was not aware. He refers to this as the "terrifying episode" with his mother and her rabbi.

As an adult living in New York, he received a phone call from his cousin, a doctor, telling him that another cousin was ill in the hospital. The sick man, who was deeply religious, was in need of surgery and refused to have it until Wiesel came to the hospital to give him a blessing. (In Judaism, blessings are traditionally offered on many occasions, and one such time is during severe illness.) Wiesel immediately traveled to the hospital, but he hesitated to offer his blessing to his cousin, believing that his cousin was much more religious than Wiesel himself was. But because his cousin insisted and continued to refuse the necessary surgery, he relented and offered the blessing. When his cousin was recovering from successful surgery, Wiesel raised the subject again. "Why did you ask for my blessing?" His cousin explained that Wiesel's blessing was important to him because of an encounter that had happened many years before, when Wiesel was just an eight-year-old boy.

At that time, Wiesel's mother's rabbi was visiting the family in Sighet. The rabbi spent time alone with young Elie, asking him questions about his studies and talking with him about religious matters. Elie marveled at the beauty of his voice and face and enjoyed being in the man's presence. A half hour or so later the rabbi asked the boy to leave so that he could be alone with his mother. After a short while, Wiesel's mother emerged from the room, crying bitterly. Although her son constantly asked her, "Why do you cry?" she refused to answer. He was afraid that he had said or done something to insult the rabbi. For weeks he continued to ask her why, but she never told him. Eventually he forgot about the incident.

Reminding Wiesel of this encounter, the cousin explained that he also was there that day. Since he was close to Wiesel's mother, she had confided in him why she had cried. She repeated the words the rabbi spoke to her, "Sarah, daughter of David, I want you to know that one day your son will grow up to be a great man in Israel, but neither you nor I will be alive to see it." Wiesel's cousin concluded, "If the rabbi said that about you, I think that your blessing does carry weight."[3]

In 1972, Wiesel was appointed professor of Jewish studies at the City College of New York and then went on to teach humanities at Boston University in 1976. Because of his fine work, President Jimmy Carter appointed him to lead the United States Holocaust Memorial Council, an organization committed to honoring the dead, remembering the past, and educating for the future. Wiesel headed that group from 1980 to 1986.

He always knew he would one day return to Birkenau, bringing his wife Marion and son Shlomo with him. He did return, but not the way he envisioned it. While serving on the commission, he and a delegation of forty-three others, many of them also Holocaust survivors, traveled to Europe to visit the death camps in Poland and the execution sites in Russia. He returned to this "Kingdom of Night" surrounded not by family and friends, but by reporters and television cameras. About that encounter he writes:

> We were never alone. And yet each of us had never been so alone. These men and women, these survivors, remembered those they had lost as they stood at the very sites where they had disappeared. One had to be there in order to understand that there are some kinds of loneliness that can never be overcome. Only those who lived through the Event know what it was; the others will never know.[4]

Wiesel admits that the emotion of the moment was clouded by the activities that marked the occasion of their return: meetings, discussions, ceremonies. As attempts to remember the victims of Birkenau and Auschwitz continued, Wiesel reminded the attendees that the vast majority of those killed were Jews. Yes, they said to him, the victims were Poles and Jews. Just don't forget, he insisted, that only the Jews were slated for total extermination. If you forget the Jews, he said, you will eventually forget the others.

On that day, the survivors went together to the camps. Those who had been inmates at Birkenau, including Wiesel, broke away from the rest of the group. They linked arms and walked slowly across the train tracks to the gas chambers and the crematorium, to the place where their family members died. *What shall we say?* he thought. *Shall we say a prayer?* But, of course, there is no prayer for such places. Suddenly, voices were raised in song. The survivors began to sing the *Sh'ma Israel*, the ancient prayer given by God to Moses so many years ago: "Hear, O Israel, God is our God, God is one."[5]

In addition to teaching and lecturing throughout the world, Wiesel has continued to lead protests and speak out on behalf of oppressed peoples in many places, including the former Soviet

Union, Cambodia, Biafra, Bangladesh, and Latin America. On many occasions, he has successfully interceded with various world leaders to encourage a more compassionate stance toward those who suffer. Even unsuccessful attempts have not deterred him from speaking out when he deems it necessary.

For example, in April 1985 he received the Congressional Gold Medal of Achievement from then President Ronald Reagan. Wiesel made use of the opportunity to persuade the President not to carry out a planned visit to a cemetery in Bitburg, then located in West Germany. Many members of the infamous German SS are buried in that cemetery, and Wiesel believed that such a visit would dishonor the memory of those who were ruthlessly murdered by the Nazis. In his acceptance speech Wiesel said:

> Allow me, Mr. President, to touch on a matter which is sensitive. I belong to a traumatized generation; to us symbols are important. Following our ancient tradition which commands us to "speak truth to power," may I speak to you of the recent events that have caused us much pain and anguish?

> We have met four or five times. I know of your commitment to humanity. I am convinced that you were not aware of the presence of SS graves in the Bitburg cemetery. But now we all are aware of that presence. I therefore implore you, Mr. President, in the spirit of this moment that justifies so many others, tell us now that you will not go there: *that* place is not your place. Your place is with the *victims* of the SS.[6]

Despite this impassioned plea, the President made the trip.

In 1986 Wiesel was awarded the Nobel Peace Prize in a ceremony in Oslo, Norway. Honored for his vast writings about the Holocaust and his continuing efforts on behalf of oppressed peoples and political prisoners everywhere, Wiesel insisted that he shared the award with all Jewish survivors. He took some moments to remember the young boy he was in Sighet and Birkenau, and the man he was to become. The boy asked the man, "'What have you done with my future? What have you done with your life?' And I tell him that I have tried. That I have tried to keep memory alive, that I have tried to fight those who would forget. Because if we forget, we are guilty, we are accomplices."[7] Even today, the questions he asks and the stories he tells challenge those who hear to think more deeply about God and God's relationship to the world, about human nature and people's responsibility to each other, and about the importance of remembering the witness of those who have gone before us.

READ THE WORDS

As you read the works that follow, ask yourself these questions: What are some ways in which Wiesel's writings connect to his life story? How do these words nurture my spiritual life and/or inspire me to engage in acts of social justice?

READING ONE:

The novel with which Wiesel broke his ten-year silence was the autobiographical Night. *It is an excellent starting place for an introduction to the issues that carry through all of his later writings.*

The summer was coming to an end. The Jewish year was nearly over.

On the eve of Rosh Hashanah, the last day of the accursed year, the whole camp was electric with the tension which was in all our hearts. In spite of everything, this day was different from any other. The last day of the year. The word "last" rang very strangely. What if it were indeed the last day?

They gave us our evening meal, a very thick soup, but no one touched it. We wanted to wait until after prayers. At the place of assembly, surrounded by the electrified barbed wire, thousands of silent Jews gathered, their faces stricken.

Night was falling. Other prisoners continued to crowd in, from every block, able suddenly to conquer time and space and submit both to their will.

"What are You, my God," I thought angrily, "compared to this afflicted crowd, proclaiming to You their faith, their anger, their revolt? What does Your greatness mean, Lord of the universe, in the face of all this weakness, this decomposition, and this decay? Why do You still trouble their sick minds, their crippled bodies?"

The thousand men had come to attend the solemn service, heads of the blocks, Kapos, functionaries of death.

"Bless the Eternal..."

The voice of the officiant had just made itself heard. I thought at first it was the wind.

"Blessed be the Name of the Eternal!"

Thousands of voices repeated the benediction; thousands of men prostrated themselves like trees before a tempest.

"Blessed be the Name of the Eternal!"

Why, but why should I bless Him? In every fiber I rebelled. Because He had thousands of children burned in His pits? Because He kept six crematories working night and day, on Sundays and feast days? Because in His great might He had created Auschwitz, Birkenau, Buna, and so many factories of death? How could I say to Him: "Blessed art Thou, Eternal, Master of the Universe, Who chose us from among the races to be tortured day and night, to see our fathers, our mothers, our brothers, end in the crematory? Praised be Thy Holy Name, Thou Who hast chosen us to be butchered on Thine altar?"

I heard the voice of the officiant rising up, powerful yet at the same time broken, amid the tears, sobs, the sighs of the whole congregation:

"All the earth and the Universe are God's!"

He kept stopping every moment, as though he did not have the strength to find the meaning beneath the words. The melody choked in his throat.

And I, mystic that I had been, I thought:

"Yes, man is very strong, greater than God. When you were deceived by Adam and Even, you drove them out of Paradise. When Noah's generation displeased You, You brought down the flood. When Sodom no longer found favor in Your eyes, You made the sky rain down fire and sulphur. But these men here, whom You have betrayed, whom You have allowed to be tortured, butchered, gassed, burned, what do they do? They pray before You! They praise Your name!

"All creation bears witness to the Greatness of God!"

Once, New Year's Day had dominated my life. I knew that my sins grieved the Eternal; I implored his forgiveness. Once, I had believed profoundly that upon one solitary deed of mine, one solitary prayer, depended the salvation of the world.

This day I had ceased to plead. I was no longer capable of lamentation. On the contrary, I felt very strong. I was the accuser,

God the accused. My eyes were open and I was alone—terribly alone in a world without God and without man. Without love or mercy. I had ceased to be anything but ashes, yet I felt myself to be stronger than the Almighty, to whom my life had been tied for so long. I stood amid that praying congregation, observing it like a stranger.

The service ended with the Kaddish. Everyone recited the Kaddish over his parents, over his children, over his brothers, and over himself.

We stayed for a long time at the assembly place. No one dared to drag himself away from this mirage. Then it was time to go to bed and slowly the prisoners made their way over to their blocks. I heard people wishing one another a Happy New Year!

I ran off to look for my father. And at the same time I was afraid of having to wish him a Happy New Year when I no longer believed in it.

He was standing near the wall, bowed down, his shoulders sagging as though beneath a heavy burden. I went up to him, took his hand and kissed it. A tear fell upon it. Whose was that tear? Mine? His? I said nothing. Nor did he. We had never understood each other so clearly.

The sound of the bell jolted us back to reality. We must go to bed. We came back from far away. I raised my eyes to look at my father's face leaning over mine, to try to discover a smile or something resembling one upon the aged, dried-up countenance. Nothing. Not the shadow of an expression. Beaten.[8]

READING TWO:

Published in 1978, A Jew Today *is a series of essays, reflections, and dialogues. The following excerpt is from a chapter entitled "A Plea for the Survivors."*

Time does *not* heal all wounds; there are those that remain painfully open. How can one forget the passion, the violence a simple crust of moldy bread can inspire? Or the near-worship evoked by a slightly better dressed, better nourished, less beaten inmate? How can one repress the memory of the indifference one had felt toward the corpses? Will you ever know what it is like to wake up under a frozen sky, on a journey toward the unknown, and to record without surprise that the man in front of you is dead, as is the one before him and the one behind you? Suddenly a thought crosses one's mind: What if I, I too, am already dead and do not know it? And this thought also is registered with indifference. Will you ever know the nature of a world where, as in Moses' time in the desert, the living and the dead are no longer separate? Will you ever know what a survivor knows?[9]

READING THREE:

The Six Days of Destruction *is a series of meditations on the creation story, Genesis 1:1–31. Using a literary vehicle often used in Hebrew scripture, Wiesel parallels the biblical creation account and stories from the Holocaust.*

THE FIFTH DAY

When these events are known, they will become part of the eternal legend of the people Israel. Thanks to them, we will return to the source of our memory filled with sadness and pain, but also with fidelity and pride.

For it came to pass in those days: in a ghetto in the East, a dozen young Jews were gathered in a secret meeting place lit by a dirty, dust-covered light bulb. Tense and excited, they listened, sometimes incredulously, to their leader Yehuda, who told them of the battle to come.

"Our families are dead," Yehuda said hoarsely. "Our teachers are dead. Our friends are dead. We will soon be the last members of the community, the last Jews alive in this land. Then it will be our turn. Be prepared: our honour is at stake."

They were very young fighters. Yehuda, the oldest, was twenty. The others were younger. Teenagers with the eyes and gestures of old men. Among them were workers, Yeshiva students, a carpenter, a schoolboy.

"We are going to fight," said Yehuda. "The enemy only recognizes force. We will meet his force with ours."

His comrades accepted the argument. Yehuda was right: the enemy hates our physical weakness. They kill the sick. They detest our spiritual power. They mock our intellectuals. Only the strong, the workers, have the right to live, say the enemies. Fine. We will be strong, well trained and well equipped. And will we win? Of course not; we cannot win. Yehuda and his group are aware of this. How could they defeat the strongest army in Europe? There comes a time when logic must be discarded, when you have to fight logic.

"Action," said Yehuda. "That will be our watchword. We are going to arm ourselves and resist."

"With what?" asked a timid voice.

"With…this!" said Yehuda. And he brought "this" out of his pocket: a revolver. Someone stepped back in terror. He had never seen a revolver except in the hands of killers.

"It cost its weight in gold," said Yehuda.

The training period began: how to hold the weapon, at what height, with a finger on the trigger. Keep calm; it is important to keep calm. Do not panic, do not get impatient, do not move until the target is clearly in your sights. And then…

One of them, Yerachmiel, was clumsy and ashamed of it. It was not his fault. He had never handled any weapon but the Torah. In hiding, he still studied the Talmud. Seeing his lips move in silent prayer, one understood that Yerachmiel was not made to use revolvers.

"Yehuda," he said. "Do you intend to defeat the German army with this revolver?"

"We will have more," said Yehuda.

"How many? Ten? Twenty? A hundred?"

Yehuda was silent for a long moment. That very night, or the night before, or the one after, that same discussion was going on in Bialystock and Vilna, Warsaw and Lublin, wherever Jews were oppressed, persecuted, and decimated by the enemy.

The resistance movements in occupied Europe all received aid from the Free World. The others were sent messengers and instructors, money and weapons, radio equipment and materials for sabotage; their safety was a matter of concern. Links were maintained with those units; each one was supported. Why, Lord, did they discriminate against the *Jewish* fighters? Why were they doomed to oblivion, even contempt?

Here and there, warm-hearted men and women of goodwill had certainly taken up the Jewish cause. Some risked their lives to protect and feed them and to warn them of the dangers that lay ahead. But they were few...few and rare.[10]

READING FOUR:

In 1986 Wiesel received the Nobel Peace Prize. In the following excerpt from his acceptance address, we see his concern for the alleviation of oppression worldwide.

Of course, since I am a Jew profoundly rooted in my people's memory and tradition, my first response is to Jewish fears, Jewish needs, Jewish crises. For I belong to a traumatized generation, one that experienced the abandonment and solitude of our people. It would be unnatural for me not to make Jewish priorities my own: Israel, Soviet Jewry, Jews in Arab lands...But others are important to me. Apartheid is, in my view, as abhorrent as anti-Semitism. To me, Andrei Sakharov's isolation is as much a disgrace as Josef Begun's imprisonment and Ida Nudel's exile. As is the denial of Solidarity and its leader Lech Walesa's right to dissent. And Nelson Mandela's interminable imprisonment.

There is so much injustice and suffering crying out for our attention: victims of hunger, of racism and political persecution—in Chile, for instance, or in Ethiopia—writers and poets, prisoners in so many lands governed by the Left and by the Right.

Human rights are being violated on every continent. Many more people are oppressed than free. How can one not be sensitive to their plight? Human suffering anywhere concerns men and women everywhere.[11]

REFLECT AND ACT

By yourself, or in cooperation with others, engage in the following reflection and action exercises. Try to do one exercise each day for a week. If one activity is particularly meaningful, stay with it for a longer period of time. Also feel free to create exercises of your own as you are inspired by the life and witness of Elie Wiesel.

1. Engage in playful storytelling: Read a story to a child, tell one to a friend, write one in your journal. Be as descriptive as possible: What are the sights and sounds associated with the story? What clothes are the characters wearing? How

do they feel? What do they say? Reflect on the experience: How does the activity enrich your understanding of the story?

2. Dwell on the importance of memory. Recall important memories that are either painful or joyful for you. Make time this week to call, write, or visit those people or places that hold special memories for you. What will you say to them?

3. Imagine yourself as the child you once were. What were your interests, fears, hopes, and dreams? Bring that child into conversation with the adult you have become. Answer Wiesel's questions: "What have you done with my future? What have you done with your life?"

4. Think about those issues about which you are most passionate. Why are they important to you? What do you do to nurture these passions in your life? Are you doing enough, or do you need to do more? Make the commitment to carry out one action this week.

5. Bring to mind those who are suffering or oppressed in your community, in the nation, or in other parts of the world. How can you stand in solidarity with them? Engage in some liberating activity: feed the hungry, write to legislative officials, visit someone in the hospital or in prison.

6. Pray with the daily newspaper. Look for instances of suffering and signs of God's hope and healing.

7. Have you ever spoken out publicly about something you felt was wrong or unjust? How did it feel to do that? What was the response of those who heard you? What feelings and responses did you experience in the weeks and months that followed? Would you do it again? Why or why not?

8. Remember a piece of music that brings forth strong emotions in you. Listen again to that piece and write some prose, a poem, or a letter to the composer expressing the emotions you experience.

9. With one or more friends, watch a movie or documentary about the Holocaust. Discuss and meditate on the following questions: Where was God in the midst of that awful time in history? How does the occurrence of the Holocaust affect the way in which you think about God and about human

beings? What should be your active response to this reality in our world?

10. Look again at Wiesel's acceptance speech for the Nobel Peace Prize. How has the world changed since he gave that talk in 1986? Where are human rights being violated in the world today? Read up on one area of the world and choose one thing you can do to alleviate suffering there.

FOR FURTHER READING

Brown, Robert McAfee. *Elie Wiesel: Messenger to All Humanity.* Notre Dame: University of Notre Dame Press, 1983.

Cargas, Harry James. *Harry James Cargas in Conversation with Elie Wiesel.* New York: Paulist Press, 1976.

Wiesel, Elie. *Night.* New York: Hill and Wang, 1960. (Reprint: New York: Bantam Doubleday Dell Publishing Group, 1982.)

———. *The Gates of the Forest.* New York: Avon Books, 1967.

———. *A Jew Today.* Translated by Marion Wiesel. New York: Vintage Books, 1978.

———. *From the Kingdom of Memory.* New York: Summit Books, 1990.

——— and Albert A. Friedlander. *Six Days of Destruction: Meditations towards Hope.* Oxford: Pergamon, 1988.

Notes

[1] Elie Wiesel, *The Gates of the Forest* (New York: Avon Books, 1967), 6–9.

[2] Elie Wiesel, *Night* (New York: Hill and Wang Press, 1960; reprint, New York: Bantam Doubleday Dell, 1982), 32.

[3] Harry James Cargas, *Harry James Cargas in Conversation with Elie Wiesel* (New York: Paulist Press, 1976), 73–75.

[4] Elie Wiesel, *From the Kingdom of Memory* (New York: Summit Books, 1990), 108.

[5] Ibid., 105–17.

[6] Ibid., 176.

[7] Ibid., 232–33.

[8] Wiesel, *Night,* 63–65.

[9] Elie Wiesel "A Plea for the Survivors," in *A Jew Today,* trans. Marion Wiesel (New York: Vintage Books, 1978), 222.

[10] Elie Wiesel and Albert A. Friedlander, *Six Days of Destruction: Meditations towards Hope* (Oxford: Pergamon, 1988), 37–39.

[11] Wiesel, "The Nobel Address," in *From the Kingdom of Memory,* 233–34.

Chapter Four

Marian Wright Edelman

All Children Are Our Children

Sit comfortably and quietly. Light a candle and/or play some meditative music. Close your eyes and visualize the image of a child. This child can be someone you do or do not know well, a child who lives nearby or in a foreign country. When a detailed picture has formed in your mind, ask the child, "What are your hopes for the future? What are your fears? What limits you? What can I do to help?"

HEAR THE STORIES

Marian Wright Edelman is a familiar face throughout Washington, D.C., and especially in the halls of Congress. As the head of the Children's Defense Fund, she campaigns, lobbies, and advocates on behalf of the voiceless constituents—the children of our nation. Her inclination to dedicate herself to a life of service was shaped early in her life growing up in Bennettsville, South Carolina. Born in 1939, she was the youngest of Arthur and Maggie Wright's five children. An excellent student, she also played piano and sang and was a drum majorette.

As a black girl growing up in a small town in the racially segregated South, Edelman remembers that black people could neither use the local parks nor eat at neighborhood soda shops. Likewise, a community pool was reserved for the white children, while the black children swam in a polluted river. Despite an external world that excluded blacks and said that they were less than whites, the people around her—her parents, preachers, and teachers—nurtured an internal understanding that she was a child of God and that what she did with her life really did matter.

Her father was a Baptist minister who had a sense of social mission that acted as a model for his daughter's future untiring work on behalf of children. He opened a playground and gathering place for blacks behind his own home. He also established the first home for aged blacks, in which each member of the Wright family had a job, such as administration, cleaning, or cooking.

She remembers that her childhood home was always full of books and magazines: works by Mark Twain, Carl Sandburg, Gandhi, Harry Emerson Fosdick, Paul Tillich, Reinhold Niebuhr, Benjamin Mays, Howard Thurman, W. E. B. DuBois, James Weldon Johnson, and Langston Hughes. Her father's study was also decorated with pictures of and newspaper clippings about provocative people of all races and religions. Wanting to expose his children to some of the greatest black minds and talents, he would take them to hear black singers, poets, preachers, and lecturers. Sometimes they would drive for several hours to reach a lecture hall where they would sit for three- and four-hour lectures. She still remembers one talk by Mary McLeod Bethune, the great black educator who worked to improve opportunities for black students. She told stories of segregation and of going into white retail stores to try on hats. When she was rebuffed by white store clerks, she replied, "Do you know who I am? I am Mary McLeod Bethune!"

The one thing her father valued almost as much as prayer was reading. When her older brothers and sisters had grown up and she was the only child left at home, she would sit with her father every night, reading in front of the fireplace. She recalls that once when she was a teenager she tried to trick him by inserting a copy of the racy magazine *True Confessions* inside a *Life* magazine that she pretended to read. She was found out when he asked her to read her magazine aloud and comment on its value. Embarrassed, she never had any interest in reading such material again.[1]

Edelman was fourteen years old when her father died from a heart attack. Even in the last hours of his life, he continued to encourage his children with the words, "We are not alone. God is here." His last words to her in the ambulance on the way to the hospital made a strong impression: "Don't let anything get between you and your education." During the night she was awakened by his final, labored breaths. Gathering her mother and siblings to his bedside, she remembers the peaceful expression on his face that told her all was well. Many years later, she was present for her mother's last days as well. She watched as her mother, still smiling, slipped into a coma as Marian read Psalm 103: "Bless the LORD, O my soul, and all that is within me, bless his holy name," and Psalm 27: "The LORD is my light and my salvation; whom shall I fear?" As Maggie took her final breaths, her children sang her into the heavenly home.

After the funeral, Edelman went to her mother's home to put away her things. She was amazed to discover that the very issues to which she had dedicated her life's work were well-represented among the scores of clippings, letters, magazines, and scraps her parents had collected throughout their lives. They had articles on teenage pregnancy and the need for equality in education. She also reread her father's sermons, in which he often spoke about a Christian response to the breakdown of the family. Even more amazing was her discovery of an old *Christian Century* magazine containing a quote from Dwight Eisenhower that her father had underlined in red. She had chosen this same quote decades later herself for a Children's Defense Fund poster:

> Every gun that is made, every warship launched, every rocket fired signifies a theft from those who hunger and are not fed, those who are cold and not clothed. This world in arms is not spending money alone. It is spending the sweat of its laborers, the genius of its scientists, the hope of its children.[2]

After high school Edelman went to Spelman College, the well-respected liberal arts college for women in Atlanta. The recipient of several scholarships, she was able to study in Paris, Geneva, and Moscow during her junior year in preparation for a career in foreign service. When she returned to Atlanta in the late 1950s, the civil rights movement was gaining speed. During her early years at Spelman she had been inspired by the words of activists, preachers, and educators who had visited the campus. She remembers listening to Martin Luther King, Jr., Whitney Young, Howard Thurman, and Benjamin Mays as each, in his own way, told the Spelman students that the privilege of their education carried with it the responsibility to make the world a better place. Motivated by their words as well as her parents' witness, she participated in the famous sit-ins at Atlanta's city hall and even asked her friends to picket. For picketing, she spent a night in jail.

Deeply touched by the vast suffering of people of color in the United States, she abandoned her plans to enter foreign service and instead entered Yale Law School. She hoped that through the knowledge and practice of law she could improve the lives of blacks. Graduating in 1963, she began an internship with the National Association for the Advancement of Colored People (NAACP) in New York, where she learned how to prepare trial briefs specifically for civil rights cases. Having had this invaluable experience, she chose to go to Mississippi to practice law since, at that time, the state had 900,000 blacks and only three black lawyers. Edelman became the first black woman to be admitted to the law bar in that state.

Mississippi was also a hotbed of activity in the struggle for civil rights. When she arrived there in 1964, the Mississippi Summer Project was in full swing. Thousands of white college students from northern schools had converged on the state to register black voters. In those early days, most of her time was spent getting young people out of jail, many of whom had been badly beaten by police and segregationists. She also turned her attention to dealing with the relentless poverty that characterized the lives of blacks in the south. She realized quickly that unless people's lives could be improved economically, the hard-won gains of the civil rights movement would not have much positive effect on them.

Edelman remembers a particularly poignant moment in April 1968, on the day that Martin Luther King, Jr., was assassinated. The anger and frustration among blacks was strong and deadly.

In Jackson, Mississippi, she came across several teenagers preparing to loot and burn the city. She attempted to dissuade them, warning them that the consequences of their actions would be detrimental to their futures. "Lady," one young man replied, "I ain't got no future." Shocked by his defeatism and hopelessness, she decided then and there to dedicate herself to the cause of children and to creating a world where a young person would never have to believe that he had no future.[3]

Edelman's first work with the federal legal system was as counsel to the Child Development Group of Mississippi. She watched with disbelief as legislators from Mississippi successfully argued *against* the federally funded Head Start program for underprivileged preschoolers, most of whom were black. She subsequently convinced Washington lawmakers to restore funding for the desperately needed programs, but she realized then that children had no one to speak for them in the nation's capital. While all sorts of special-interest groups had people who could go to Congress and plead their cases, children did not vote and therefore could not speak for themselves. Here the seeds were planted for the creation of the Children's Defense Fund ten years later.

Edelman's ability to influence with her actions as well as her words is well known. In 1967, for example, New York senator Robert Kennedy made a trip to Mississippi. While there, Edelman took him and members of the Senate committee on employment, manpower and poverty on a tour of the Delta shanties in which most blacks lived. These dwellings lacked electricity, heat, and running water. In one such home they came upon a small child whose stomach was distended due to hunger. Senator Kennedy, a devoted family man, knelt down to play with the young child. The child, however, was so lethargic that, despite the senator's attempts to communicate with the child, there was no response. Obviously distraught and angry over the plight of children in squalid conditions such as these, Kennedy returned to Washington determined to make the elimination of poverty a priority.[4]

One member of Kennedy's entourage was a handsome, Harvard-trained lawyer named Peter Edelman. He and his future wife found that they shared many of the same convictions and concerns. They were married in 1968 and settled in Washington,

D.C. This new locale gave Marian Wright Edelman the opportunity to pursue her dream of advocating on behalf of the poor in the nation's capital. There she created the Washington Research Project, a public interest research and advocacy group. Her greatest concern was the expansion of Head Start so that more children could receive even greater benefits. In 1973 she began the Children's Defense Fund (CDF), the organization that she continues to head today. Its aim is to give voice to the needs and concerns of children, which it does by engaging in research on issues related to the care and survival of children, providing public education on these issues, monitoring federal agencies about how well they provide for the needs of children, assisting with the drafting of legislation, and giving testimony before lawmakers. The topics CDF addresses are manifold: the treatment of institutionalized children, juvenile justice, the use of children in medical experiments, immunization, infant mortality, homelessness, teenage pregnancy, support for single-parent households, education, and the need to provide a safety net for those hurt through welfare reform.

The Edelmans have three sons: Joshua Robert, Jonah Martin, and Ezra Benjamin. As a biracial and interfaith family, they have faced challenges of their own. Because Marian is a black Christian and Peter is a white Jew, these parents have sought to pass on a combined faith and heritage. They have dealt with their own integration with characteristic grace, giving to each of their three sons his own "Baptist Bar Mitzvah." On each occasion, friends from both Jewish and Christian traditions joined together to witness the time-honored ceremony while either Grandma Wright or one of Edelman's brothers read from Psalm 139:

> O LORD, you have searched me and known me…
> Where can I go from your spirit?
>> Or where can I flee from your presence?…
> For it was you who formed my inward parts;
>> you knit me together in my mother's womb.
> I praise you, for I am fearfully and wonderfully made.
>> Psalm 139:1, 7, 13–14

These beautiful words affirm not only God's presence in their sons' lives, but the presence of those family members who are no longer of this world, particularly Marian's father, whose last sermon was on Psalm 139. She firmly believes that their sons' mixed religious and racial heritage is a gift, not a liability. She writes, "What unites us is far greater than what divides us as families and friends and Americans and spiritual sojourners on this Earth."[5]

Edelman is a humble woman of prayer and service to others who is painfully aware every time she sits in church of how often she fails to fulfill the standards modeled by her parents and the expectations she sets for herself. Although her parents are both deceased now, she continues to feel their presence closely as part of "the great cloud of witnesses" described in Hebrews 12:1. When she gets together with her sister and brothers, an important part of their talk is sharing stories with their parents as if they are present with them. She confesses to looking to the example and witness of her parents whenever she herself has a crucial decision to make.[6]

Prayer and meditation are an integral part of Edelman's life, something ingrained in her from the early days of her life when daily churchgoing was a given in her home and neighborhood. She tells of being in the hills of Bellagio, Italy, overlooking Lake Como in 1989. In that beautiful place she became strongly aware of the spiritual heritage left to her by her devout parents. The spiritual strength they imparted to her and her siblings was enough to encourage and carry them through even the most difficult of times. When the going is rough and she does not know how to proceed, she can hear her father gently humming the black spiritual "There is a balm in Gilead to make the wounded whole./ There is a balm in Gilead to heal the sin-sick soul." She writes, "My parents' example and messages keep me grounded when I am tempted to lose sight of what is important amidst mounting demands of work and family and a culture that values things and style and packaging and publicity over substance and vision and service and concrete action."[7]

In the end, Marian Wright Edelman is a dedicated children's advocate, calling children "God's presence, promise, and hope for humankind."[8] Whenever she is discouraged about the future or questions whether her work is making a difference in children's lives, she recalls the conditions under which she grew up. Neither her parents nor the other adults in her life had any promise that the segregation of the 1940s and 1950s would be eradicated. But what they did have was hope. She, like her parents, clings to the hope that the determination and prayer that she brings to her work will take root and grow, making a better life for the children of the twenty-first century.

READ THE WORDS

As you read the works that follow, ask yourself these questions: What are some ways in which Edelman's writings connect to her life story? How do these words nurture my spiritual life and/or inspire me to engage in acts of social justice?

READING ONE:

Edelman wrote The Measure of Our Success *out of concern for the future of our nation's children. The two sections of the book entitled "Letter to My Sons" and "Twenty-Five Lessons for Life" were written as "a spiritual and family dowry" in anticipation of her eldest son's twenty-first birthday. In this first selection, which is from her letter to her three sons, she reminds them that self-worth is based on something much deeper than skin color, religious affiliation, achievement, or power.*

Gandhi advised: "Let our first act every morning be the following resolve: 'I shall not fear anyone on earth. I shall fear only God. I shall bear ill-will towards no one. I shall not submit to injustice from anyone.'" No one, Eleanor Roosevelt said, can make you feel inferior without your consent. *Never* give it. Respect other people only on the basis of their individual character and personal efforts, struggles, and achievements. Never defer to another on the basis of his or her race, religion, gender, class, fame, wealth or position. Whites did not create Blacks. Men did not create women nor Christians Jews. What then gives any human being the presumption to judge, diminish or exclude another or expect deference solely on such bases? It does not take character, intellect or talent to inherit a million dollars or to be born white or male. Why should more admiration be given to those who started life with far more advantages and supports than those with none or few? No person has the right to rain on your dreams. No person has a right to define you on the basis of what you have or what you look like.

Affirm who you are inside regardless of the world's judgments: God's and my very precious children who are loved unconditionally, not for what you do, look like or own, but simply because you are a gift of a loving God. As parents we often forget to convey this, and I have been as guilty as any, as you well know. Many young people feel, as you have, so much pressure to achieve, to get top grades, high test scores, and good jobs, and to perform well in nonacademic ventures—all of which are important for acquiring the self-discipline needed to improve your life choices. But it is important for us overly perfectionist parents to make clear that you are far more than your SATs, good grades and trophies. However desirable these achievements are and however proud we are of them, they have no bearing on your intrinsic value or on our love for and acceptance of you as a person. No awards can ever rival the countless little and big joys you have given and continue to give us.[9]

READING TWO:

The second half of Edelman's "spiritual and family dowry" is a marvelous collection of wisdom and advice compiled from her years of experience as daughter, mother, wife, activist, and woman of faith. Here in Lesson 21 from her "Twenty-Five Lessons for Life" is a glimpse of the deep spiritual roots she passes along to her children.

Listen for "the sound of the genuine" within yourself and others. Meditate and learn to be alone without being lonely. "Small," Einstein said, "is the number of them that see with their own eyes and feel with their own hearts." Try to be one of them. "There is," Howard Thurman told Spelman College students in 1981, "something in every one of you that waits and listens for the sound of the genuine in yourself." It is "the only true guide you'll ever have. And if you cannot hear it, you will all of your life spend your days on the ends of strings somebody else pulls."

There are so many noises and pulls and competing demands in our lives that many of us never find out who we are. Learn to be quiet enough to hear the sound of the genuine within yourself so that you can hear it in other people.

It is as necessary as it is hard to practice a regular discipline of silence, solitude or prayer. I have not fully succeeded but I cannot survive long without my moments. A few minutes every hour, a half hour or hour every day, a day a month, a week a year—in dedicated silence—is a goal to pursue. Even better is the attainment of an internal quiet space within yourself amidst never-ceasing external bedlam. It's tempting to hide behind a too-busy life as an excuse to avoid solitude, and in this I am guiltier than most. But each of us can do what we *really* want to do. St. Francis de Sales recounted how, when St. Catherine of Siena's parents deprived her of time and place to pray and meditate, she simply created a cell within her own heart to dwell in. "The time of business," Brother Lawrence wrote, "does not differ with me from the time of prayer; and in the voice and clatter of my kitchen, while several persons are at the same time calling for different things, I possess God in as great tranquillity as if I were on my knees at the Blessed Sacrament." I wish I could say this of myself, and I heed Gandhi's warning that the world will never be saved if we have to withdraw in order to gain inner peace and balance.[10]

READING THREE:

In 1986, Edelman delivered the W. E. B. DuBois Lectures at Harvard University on which her book Families in Peril *is based. She tells of the vast suffering of children in our country, with black children and the children of teenage mothers faring the worst. She calls on American leaders and caring adults everywhere to engage in compassionate action, something long characteristic of the black community.*

Albert Einstein believed the world to be in greater peril from those who tolerate evil than from those who commit it. Democracy is not a spectator sport. I worry about people who opt out of political, bureaucratic and community processes, even while I recognize that those processes are sometimes discouraging. I worry about men and women who refuse to take a position because of the complexity or controversy that often surround issues of life and death. I hold no brief for those who are content to kibitz intellectually about the life choices of millions of poor children without seeing the hunger and suffering behind the cold statistics, or for those who hide behind professional neutrality and shift responsibility for hard society problems on to others—problems that must be shared if they are to be solved.

Feeding a hungry child or preventing needless infant deaths in a decent, rich society should not require detailed policy analysis or quantifiable outcome goals or endless commissions. They require compassionate action. By all means let us have more careful definition and justification for our policy goals and spending. Let us apply the same cost-benefit standards consistently to the military and to programs for the nonpoor. But let us be careful not to hide behind cost-benefit analyses when human survival is at issue.

Each of us must reflect hard within ourselves, our families, our churches, synagogues, universities and home communities, about the national ideals we want America to hold. Each of us must then try "little by little," as Dorothy Day recognized, to live them and be moved to act in the personal arena through greater service to those around us who are more needy, and in the political arena to ensure a more just society. One without the other is not enough to transform the United States.[11]

READING FOUR:
Guide My Feet is a book of prayers, litanies, and reflections, most of which were written by Edelman herself. This first prayer is a reminder that merely because something is legal in the eyes of the judicial system does not automatically make it just and right in the eyes of God.

O God, forgive our rich nation where small babies die of cold quite legally.

O God, forgive our rich nation where small children suffer from hunger quite legally.

O God, forgive our rich nation where toddler and school children die from guns sold quite legally.

O God, forgive our rich nation that lets children be the poorest group of citizens quite legally.

O God, forgive our rich nation that lets the rich continue to get more at the expense of the poor quite legally.

O God, forgive our rich nation which thinks security rests in missiles rather than in mothers, and in bombs rather than in babies.

O God, forgive our rich nation for not giving You sufficient thanks by giving to others their daily bread.

O God, help us never to confuse what is quite legal
with what is just and right in Your sight.[12]

READING FIVE:

This prayer from Guide My Feet *offers a glimpse of Edelman's
unswerving commitment to hear and follow the will of God.*

O God, help me to feel Your presence
everywhere I go today.
To see You in everyone I meet today.
To sense You in all I hear today.
To reflect You in all I do today.
To pray to and trust You in all I experience today.
To struggle to be like You in all I am today.
To speak of and for You in all I say today.
To thank You for everything every day.[13]

READING SIX:

*"A Celebration of God's Diverse Universe" demonstrates that the joy
of recognizing diversity is a gracious gift from a good and loving
God.*

O God of the blue, red, brown, black and multicolored bird,
of the singing, humming and silent bird, of the noisy woodpecker
and the cooing dove, of perfect yellow sunflowers, fanciful pan-
sies and pungent purple lavender, thank You for Your beautiful
gifts of rich difference and variety.

O God, whose countless shades of green we cannot discern,
who made no two leaves, grasses, animals or humans alike, who
made blue sky, white and gray clouds, soft reddish-brown and
black earthen soils, infinite desert sands and impenetrable oceans
deep, we thank You for the manifold and diverse universe You
have made and shared with us.[14]

REFLECT AND ACT

*By yourself, or in cooperation with others, engage in the following
reflection and action exercises. Try to do one exercise each day for a
week. If one activity is particularly meaningful, stay with it for a*

longer period of time. Also feel free to create exercises of your own as you are inspired by the life and witness of Marian Wright Edelman.

1. Remember your childhood, specifically the ways in which you were challenged to do your best by the adults in your life. Who were your cheerleaders? Did you feel overly pressured by them, ignored by them, or somewhere in between? If you are a parent or are in a position to lend support to a child, consider how the children in your life would answer these questions.

2. In Reading Two, Edelman counsels her children to "learn to be quiet enough to hear the sound of the genuine within yourself so that you can hear it in other people." List the ways in which you listen to yourself: your mind, emotions, body, and spirit. Also list the ways in which you are attentive to the dreams, concerns, needs, and wants of others. Do you find it easier to listen to yourself or others? Reflect on Edelman's suggestion that the ability to hear others depends on the ability to hear oneself.

3. In Edelman's life story there are several turning points, crucial moments that profoundly shaped how she would carry out God's work in the world. Look again at her story and find those moments, reflecting on how they affected her. Where have important turning points occurred in your life, in the history of your religious tradition, in your community or nation, and in our world?

4. Do you, like Edelman, have difficulty finding time for solitude? What gets in the way of making time for prayer? Brainstorm some ways you could create a space for silence in your life, such as taking a retreat day at a local monastery, getting up one hour earlier for prayer, or taking regular walks in the woods. Plan to incorporate one or two of your ideas into your schedule, starting today.

5. Learn about poverty or illness by looking at it through the eyes of a child. Read about a family living in an inner-city ghetto, a child living in a drought-stricken country, or a young person living with AIDS. Allow yourself to feel deeply their joy and pain, then express what you have experienced by

drawing a picture, writing a prayer or poem, composing a song, or dancing. What is one thing you could do to advocate on behalf of that person?

6. Have you experienced a significant death in your lifetime? Remember this event by recalling as many details as you possibly can: who died, where the death took place, the smells and sounds, who was present, who was missed, the events leading up to the death, what happened afterward, the reactions of other significant people in your life, and your own feelings about the loss. Do you have any regrets? Did you learn anything about that person after his/her death that you did not know beforehand? Write about the experience, perhaps in the form of a one-act play or a letter to the one who died.

7. Familiar wisdom reminds us that "an action is worth a thousand words." Reflecting on your own experience and the example of others, consider to what extent this is true. Recall stories that speak to this theme. Share them, if possible, in a small group. What characteristics do the stories have in common?

8. Think about the various religious, social, professional, and governmental communities of which you are part. What is their commitment to issues of social justice? How do these organizations address the problems of suffering in our world? Pray and meditate about the organization's response to these issues and assess its impact on them. Is there a need for a change in how these issues are addressed? Several members of one organization might find it especially meaningful to carry out this exercise in a small group.

9. Have there been times in your personal and corporate life when certain passages of sacred scripture or other religious writing held special meaning for you, perhaps during a crisis or particularly challenging time? Recall the circumstances and the passage that accompanied that time. Notice if different passages gave meaning to different times, or if one passage emerges as your life theme.

10. Read through the daily newspaper or a recent newsmagazine looking for judicial decisions that exemplify our nation's

understanding of "justice," such as the imposition of punishment on criminals, laws passed by Congress and other legislative bodies, and Supreme Court decisions. Then search the sacred scriptures of your religious tradition to uncover what guidance they provide in interpreting what you discovered in the news. How are understandings of justice shaped by religious belief and practice? How can you give an informed response to the actions of elected officials?

11. Invite each member of a small group to bring a favorite children's book. As you share the books with one another, discuss how the stories and illustrations spark the imagination and give hope and reassurance to children.

For Further Reading

Edelman, Marian Wright. *Families in Peril: An Agenda for Social Change.* Cambridge: Harvard University Press, 1987.
———. *The Measure of Our Success: A Letter to My Children and Yours.* Boston: Beacon Press, 1992.
———. *Guide My Feet: Prayers and Meditations on Loving and Working for Children.* Boston: Beacon Press, 1995.

Notes

[1] Marian Wright Edelman, *The Measure of Our Success* (Boston: Beacon Press, 1992), 60–62.
[2] Ibid., 76–77.
[3] Nancy Traver, *Time,* March 23, 1987, 27.
[4] Judith Graham, ed., *Current Biography Yearbook 1992* (New York: Wilson Company, 1992), 180.
[5] Edelman, *Measure of Our Success,* 77–78.
[6] Ibid., 75.
[7] Ibid., 17–18.
[8] Ibid., 11.
[9] Ibid., 26–27.
[10] Ibid., 69–71.
[11] Marian Wright Edelman, *Families in Peril: An Agenda for Social Change* (Cambridge: Harvard University, 1987), 101–2.
[12] Marian Wright Edelman, *Guide My Feet: Prayers and Meditations on Loving and Working for Children* (Boston: Beacon Press, 1995), 88.
[13] Ibid., 54.
[14] Ibid., 80.

Chapter Five

Thich Nhat Hanh

Easing Suffering
through Compassion for All

PREPARE TO MEDITATE

Practice five to ten minutes of Buddhist sitting meditation: Sit comfortably on a chair with feet flat on the floor. Or, if you are able, sit on a cushion on the floor in a full lotus or half-lotus position (cross-legged with one foot resting on the opposite thigh). Breathe slowly, but naturally. Allow yourself to be attentive to the present moment. If memories of yesterday or thoughts of tomorrow creep in, send them gently on their way. Always come back to your breath and the present moment. With continued practice, gradually increase meditation time to thirty minutes or an hour.

HEAR THE STORIES

Look at any photograph of Buddhist monk Thich Nhat Hanh, and you will see a smile that not only lights up his whole face but invites you to smile back at him as well. Zen master, poet, and peace activist Thich Nhat Hanh was born in Vietnam in 1926. He became a monk at the age of sixteen, at which time he took the name Nhat Hanh which means "one action." Thich is the Vietnamese equivalent of the family name of the Buddha and is the title taken by all monks and nuns as well. Most people, however, affectionately call him Thây (pronounced like "tie"), which means "teacher" in Vietnamese.

Thây knew that he wanted to become a monk when he was nine years old. Looking at a picture of the Buddha on the cover of a magazine, he saw one who was peaceful and happy. He decided he wanted to be this way as well. Six months later he and his classmates went on a trip to visit a hermit, a type of monk who spends most of his time in solitude and contemplation. At that time, Nhat Hanh had no idea what a hermit was but was excited about meeting him anyway. The children walked six miles to the mountain where the hermit lived, then walked another hour up the mountain. They were disappointed to discover, however, that the hermit was not there; they did not realize that hermits generally do not like to greet too many people.

The other children stopped for lunch, but Nhat Hanh continued up the hill hoping to find the hermit. As he was walking, he heard the sound of water dripping and came across a beautiful well. When he looked into the well, the water was so clean and clear that he could see all the way to the bottom. "I knelt down and drank the sparkling, clear water and felt completely fulfilled," he writes. "It was as if I were meeting the hermit face to face!" Exhausted from his journey, he lay down and fell asleep. When he awoke with a start sometime later, he was disoriented and wondered why he was lying on the hillside. Quickly realizing where he was, he hurried down the mountain to meet up with his classmates. A sentence came to his mind; curiously, it was not in Vietnamese, but in French: "*J'ai goûté l'eau la plus délicieuse du monde.*" ("I have tasted the most delicious water in the world.") While the other children played, Nhat Hanh ate his lunch in silence, thinking only of the hermit and the well.[1]

Upon joining the monastery at sixteen years of age, he began the rigorous training of a Buddhist monk, but found that much of it was old-fashioned and needed to be updated for modern times. Although he made this suggestion to his teachers, they failed to take him seriously. Thus, he and some other monks left the monastery to live in an abandoned temple in Saigon. There they studied Western philosophy and science in the hope of infusing the ancient teachings of Buddhism with contemporary principles that would make them accessible to more people. Over time they became skilled in the ancient practices of Buddhism: sitting meditation, concentrating on the breath, quieting the thoughts, and looking deeply to recognize the interconnectedness of all.

A prolific writer, Nhat Hanh published four books before he was twenty years old. In addition, he edited the magazine of the largest Buddhist organization in Vietnam during the 1940s, and wrote short stories, novels, and poetry. In the 1950s, he founded the first Buddhist high school in Vietnam. This was a significant achievement because, at the time, all secondary schools were developed according to a Western Christian model, providing no opportunities for young people to learn Buddhism and practice meditation. Continuing his quest to make Buddhism an integral part of people's lives, he then went on to form a monastery in central Vietnam dedicated to the spiritual renewal of monks, nuns, and lay people alike.

In 1961 Nhat Hanh went to the United States to study comparative religions at Princeton University and Columbia University. By 1963, however, the war in Vietnam was raging, and he was called back to his homeland by his friends, who sought his guidance and help in working for peace. Buddhist monks and nuns have a highly developed meditation life, able to sit quietly for long periods of time, stilling their thoughts and concentrating on the rhythm of the breath in the present moment. But they soon discovered that they could not continue to sit in their temples in quiet repose while those outside the temple were crying and dying. Nhat Hanh coined the term "engaged Buddhism" to describe this commitment to both meditation and helping those in need.

During the war, Nhat Hanh founded the Tiep Hien Order, also known as the Order of Interbeing, a religious order dedicated to this notion of engaged Buddhism. *Tiep* means "to be in touch," reminding members that they must be in touch with themselves through regular meditation and looking deeply with understanding and compassion. Nhat Hanh explains that unless one can offer these gifts to oneself, one is unable to extend them to others. *Hien* has two meanings. First, it means "the present time," for the present moment is all that anyone has; so now is the time for peace, joy, and compassion. Second, it means "to make real," emphasizing that love and understanding are not only concepts to be discussed but actions and attitudes that must be manifested in the world today. Nhat Hanh developed the new English word "interbeing" to express the notion that all beings are interrelated and the hope that those who are awake to this knowledge may live lives of compassion, understanding, joy, and peace. Like most religious orders, the Order of Interbeing is made up of a core group of monks and sisters, as well as an extended community of people all over the world who adhere to the order's fourteen precepts. The precepts are summarized in the following two promises: "I vow to develop my compassion in order to love and protect the life of people, animals, and plants," and "I vow to develop understanding in order to be able to love and to live in harmony with people, animals, and plants."[2]

Thây founded the School of Youth for Social Service in 1964. Monks, nuns, and college students went into the war-torn countryside to provide education and health care, and to rebuild villages destroyed by bombing, sometimes rebuilding the same village as many as eight times! What made Thây's work unique was his unwillingness to side with either faction in the war. He taught that war was the result of misunderstanding and that all people suffer because of it; he and his workers sought reconciliation, not victory. This was quite a dangerous stance for them to take, since both the Communists and anti-Communists looked upon them with suspicion. Some monks and nuns even immolated themselves, burned themselves alive, to call attention to the depth of the suffering of the people. Even then, those who did not understand thought this was just another political act and failed to hear their cries for peace.

In 1966 Nhat Hanh was invited to visit the United States and provide a firsthand account of the suffering of the Vietnamese people. There he met with Secretary of Defense Robert McNamara, Trappist monk Thomas Merton, Senators William Fulbright and Edward Kennedy, and Martin Luther King, Jr. He developed a deep friendship with King, who then began to speak out against the war in Vietnam. King nominated Nhat Hanh for the Nobel Peace Prize in 1967. From the United States, Thây went on to Europe, where he met with Pope Paul VI. Because he spoke so frankly while he was abroad, Thây was prohibited from returning to Vietnam, where he would have most certainly been imprisoned. He was offered asylum in France, and has lived there ever since.

After the war Thây sought ways to help those who were continuing to suffer in Vietnam as well as those hoping to escape from the country and make a new home elsewhere in the world. He and other members of the Order of Interbeing set up a network of underground workers who smuggled food into the country. They even tried to rescue boat people from the Gulf of Siam through a program he called *Mau Chay Ruot Mem* ("When blood is shed, we all suffer"). He did not want to repeat the unsuccessful attempts of others that always resulted in the refugees' being sent back to Vietnam or left to die in the treacherous waters of the Gulf of Siam. Therefore, Nhat Hanh and his associates, working from a location in Singapore, carried out this rescue in complete secret with the intention of taking the refugees to either Guam or Australia. Once safely there, they intended to call a press conference to bring attention to the plight of the boat people. Throughout this time, Nhat Hanh and his workers lived in a heightened state of mindfulness, sitting in meditation every day, often late into the night, chanting words of hope and courage. They knew that if they were not fully awake and aware, people would die because they had neglected their spiritual practice.

Unfortunately, someone leaked information to the press, and their plan was exposed. Singapore police surrounded his home at two o'clock in the morning, with officers blocking both back and front doors. Nhat Hanh was ordered to leave the country within twenty-four hours. He was deeply concerned for the safety of the eight hundred refugees who drifted on the sea, with little food and water and no country to take them in. He says that even though he was standing on dry land, he thought of himself as one of the refugees floating to an uncertain future on a boat with nowhere to dock.

He recalled an incident a few years before when he had written four Chinese characters on a paper lamp shade. The English translation for those characters is "If you want peace, peace is with you now." In the midst of that particularly tense twenty-four hours, he continuously meditated on those words. Likewise, he took mindful breaths and steps in order to stay aware of the present moment. He says that he found himself in a state of peace and calm, not worried or afraid. Despite the chaos of that time, he will never forget the peacefulness he experienced. In the end, however, he was forced to turn over the refugees to the United Nations High Commission on Refugees. The refugees languished in Malaysian camps for years. Although saddened by the outcome, Nhat Hanh offers a characteristically Buddhist interpretation when he says, "the conditions were not right."[3]

From there he retreated to Plum Village, a small Buddhist community in southwestern France. He remained there for five years while he entered into a period of meditation. Thây was still committed to engaged Buddhism but was perplexed about how best to proceed in his efforts. His concern for human rights abuses in Vietnam led him to continue to give courage to the monks and nuns remaining in his homeland. Government officials viewed him as such a threat that they twice spread rumors that Nhat Hanh had died. Even today his writings are smuggled back into Vietnam and are hand-copied so that they can be circulated among the people. Even though he is a refugee himself, he continues to have a strong influence in his country of origin.

His work and practice is deeply shaped by the Buddhist teaching that you must be one with what you wish to understand. This was something he had expressed most eloquently during the war when he called for an end to the fighting not because one side was more right than the other, but because war causes all to suffer. He was also able to practice this in a spiritual way when he worked for a committee that helped children who were orphaned by the war. The committee provided a photo and other information about each child so that helpers, such as Nhat Hanh, could translate the information from Vietnamese into French, English, Dutch, or German. Sponsors were then sought who could provide financial support for the children. The children were placed with family members, and the money donated on their behalf paid for food, housing, books, and clothes. Nhat Hanh had a marvelous way of "translating" the information provided to him. Instead of reading what had been written about the child, he looked deeply into the face of the photo of the child. After only thirty to forty seconds of looking at the child, he became one with the child. Then, with pen in hand, he would write the description. He says, "It was not I who had translated the application; it was the child and me, who had become one...I became him, and he became me, and together we did the translation. It was very natural."[4]

Like most Buddhists, Nhat Hanh meditates on the Three
Jewels. They are the Buddha (the teacher), the Dharma (the
teaching), and the Sangha (the community). A typical meditation is expressed by the words

> I take refuge in the Buddha,
>   the one who shows me the way in this life.
> I take refuge in the Dharma,
>   the way of understanding and love.
> I take refuge in the Sangha,
>   the community that lives in harmony and awareness.[5]

He writes of the time he was on a beach in Sri Lanka and
came across six children playing happily in the sand. He was
overjoyed to see them because they were so beautiful and happy.
He wanted to greet them but did not speak their language. Suddenly, the idea came to him to chant a prayer in the ancient
Buddhist language of Pali. He placed his hands together in the
traditional way and began to sing, "I take refuge in the Buddha…" Immediately four of the children put their palms together
and joined him in the chant. All the while the two other children
stood by silently, not wanting to participate but obviously re-
spectful of what was happening. Nhat Hanh invited them to join
the chant. They smiled, placed their hands together and began
to sing a slightly different song: "I take refuge in Mother Mary…"
These Christian children joined their Buddhist friends in prayer.
Neither differences of religion nor differences of language could
mar this sacred moment. When the chant was over, Nhat Hanh
reached out to embrace each child as an expression of the oneness he felt with them.[6]

By the early 1980s Thây returned to the United States and
began to lecture and teach Westerners the techniques of engaged Buddhism: sitting contemplation, walking meditation,
mindfulness, conscious breathing, and smiling. He has sought
ways of adapting Buddhism to Western culture, such as "telephone meditation" in which the practitioner allows the phone to
ring three times before answering it. While it rings, take time to
breathe and smile, he says. Let the phone be a reminder to be
mindful and aware of the present moment. Because Americans
do a great deal of commuting each day, Nhat Hanh also developed "driving meditation" and "subway meditation." He points

out that even though we tend to see these things as a drudgery, being mindful of these activities enables us to take more pleasure in them.[7]

Thây often returns to Plum Village and leads retreats for those wishing to become more adept at Buddhist techniques. Many of those who attend the workshops are members of Christian, Jewish, and other religious traditions. They learn principles and practices that make it possible for them to deepen their own spiritual journeys. At the conclusion of an interfaith retreat in California, for example, one man approached Nhat Hanh saying, "Thây, I feel more Jewish than ever. I will tell my rabbi that a Buddhist monk inspired me to go back to him."[8] In addition to his teaching and writing, Thich Nhat Hanh tends to his garden and works on behalf of refugees throughout the world. Through the daily practice of mindfulness and a vow to alleviate suffering, he brings compassion, understanding, and peace to our world.

READ THE WORDS

As you read the works that follow, ask yourself these questions: What are some ways in which Nhat Hanh's writings connect to his life story? How do these words nurture my spiritual life and/or inspire me to engage in acts of social justice?

READING ONE:

Being Peace is a series of talks that Thich Nhat Hanh gave to peaceworkers and meditation students during a tour of Buddhist centers in 1985. Whenever he gave these lectures, Nhat Hanh always invited the children to sit immediately in front of him. This description of what it means to be a Buddha includes an example both children and adults can understand.

The root-word *buddh* means to wake up, to know, to understand; and he or she who wakes up and understands is called a Buddha. It is as simple as that. The capacity to wake up, to understand, and to love is called Buddha nature. When Buddhists say "I take refuge in the Buddha," they are expressing trust in their own capacity of understanding, of becoming awake. The Chinese and the Vietnamese say, "I go back and rely on the

Buddha in me." Adding "in me" makes it very clear that you yourself are the Buddha...

Understanding and love are not two things, but just one. Suppose your son wakes up one morning and sees that it is already quite late. He decides to wake up his younger sister, to give her enough time to eat breakfast before going to school. It happens that she is grouchy and instead of saying, "Thank you for waking me up," she says, "Shut up! Leave me alone!" and kicks him. He will probably get angry, thinking, "I woke her up nicely. Why did she kick me?" He may want to go to the kitchen and tell you about it, or even kick her back. But then he remembers that during the night his sister coughed a lot, and he realizes that she must be sick. Maybe she has a cold, maybe that is why she behaved so meanly. He is not angry any more. At that moment there is *buddh* in him. He understands, he is awake.

When you understand, you cannot help but love. You cannot get angry. To develop understanding, you have to practice looking at all living beings with the eyes of compassion. When you understand, you love. And when you love, you naturally act in a way that can relieve the suffering of people. Someone who is awake, who knows, who understands, is called a Buddha. Buddha is in every one of us.[9]

READING TWO:

In Cultivating the Mind of Love, *Nhat Hanh intersperses teaching on the Mahayana Buddhist tradition with stories from his own spiritual development. This small excerpt is about living happily in the present moment, a theme represented in Buddhism and expressed in Nhat Hanh's life.*

We all have the tendency to struggle in our bodies and our minds. We believe that happiness is possible only in the future. The realization that we have already arrived, that we don't have to travel any further, that we are already here, can give us peace and joy. The conditions for our happiness are already sufficient. We only need to allow ourselves to be in the present moment, and we will be able to touch them. What are we looking for to be happy? Everything is already here. We do not need to put an object in front of us to run after, believing that until we get it, we cannot be happy. That object is always in the future, and we can never catch up to it. We are already in the Pure Land, the Kingdom of God. We are already a Buddha. We only need to wake up and realize we are already here.[10]

READING THREE:

Buddhist teaching stresses the interconnectedness of all living beings. A prolific poet, Nhat Hanh wrote the following poem after hearing about a twelve-year-old refugee girl who was raped by a sea pirate. She subsequently ended her life by jumping overboard. In the course of his meditation on this sad story, he came to the realization that had he been born under different circumstances, he could have become a sea pirate himself. He asks, "Can we look at each other and recognize ourselves in each other?"

PLEASE CALL ME BY MY TRUE NAMES

Do not say that I'll depart tomorrow
because even today I still arrive.

Look deeply: I arrive in every second
to be a bud on a spring branch,
to be a tiny bird, with wings still fragile,
        learning to sing in my new nest,
to be a caterpillar in the heart of a flower,
to be a jewel hiding itself in a stone.

I still arrive, in order to laugh and to cry,
        in order to fear and to hope,
the rhythm of my heart is the birth and
        death of all that are alive.

I am the mayfly metamorphosing on the
        surface of the river,
and I am the bird which, when spring comes,
        arrives in time to eat the mayfly.

I am the frog swimming happily in the
        clear water of a pond,
and I am the grass-snake who,
        approaching in silence,
        feeds itself on the frog.

I am the child in Uganda, all skin and bones,
    my legs as thin as bamboo sticks,
and I am the arms merchant, selling deadly
    weapons to Uganda.

I am the twelve-year-old girl, refugee
    on a small boat,
who throws herself into the ocean after
    being raped by a sea pirate,
and I am the pirate, my heart not yet capable
    of seeing and loving.

I am a member of the politburo, with
    plenty of power in my hands,
and I am the man who has to pay his
    "debt of blood" to my people,
dying slowly in a forced labor camp.

My joy is like spring, so warm it makes
    flowers bloom in all walks of life.
My pain is like a river of tears, so full it
    fills up the four oceans.

Please call me by my true names,
so I can hear all my cries and my laughs
    at once,
so I can see that my joy and pain are one.

Please call me by my true names,
    so I can wake up,
and so the door of my heart can be left open,
the door of compassion.[11]

READING FOUR:

Touching Peace *continues the themes of mindful breathing and living in the present moment Nhat Hanh first described in* Being Peace. *In this chapter called "Transforming Our Compost," he uses the metaphor of a flower's life to challenge us to look deeply into our own lives.*

When we look deeply at a flower, we can see that it is made entirely of non-flower elements, like sunshine, rain, soil, compost, air and time. If we continue to look deeply, we will also notice that the flower is on her way to becoming compost. If we don't notice this, we will be shocked when the flower begins to decompose. When we look deeply at the compost, we see that it is also on its way to becoming flowers, and we realize that flowers and compost "inter-are." They need each other. A good organic gardener does not discriminate against compost, because he knows how to transform it into marigolds, roses and many other kinds of flowers.

When we look deeply into ourselves, we see both flowers and garbage. Each of us has anger, hatred, depression, racial discrimination and many other kinds of garbage in us, but there is no need for us to be afraid. In the way that a gardener knows how to transform compost into flowers, we can learn the art of transforming anger, depression and racial discrimination into love and understanding. This is the work of meditation...

We may be in the habit of manifesting seeds of anger, sorrow and fear in our mind consciousness; seeds of joy, happiness and peace may not sprout up much. To practice mindfulness means to recognize each seed as it comes up from the storehouse and to practice watering the most wholesome seeds whenever possible, to help them grow stronger. During each moment that we are aware of something peaceful and beautiful, we water seeds of peace and beauty in us, and beautiful flowers bloom in our consciousness. The length of time we water a seed determines the strength of that seed. For example, if we stand in front of a tree, breathe consciously, and enjoy it for five minutes, seeds of happiness will be watered in us for five minutes, and those seeds will grow stronger. During the same five minutes, other seeds, like fear and pain, will not be watered. We have to practice this way every day.[12]

Living Buddha, Living Christ is Nhat Hanh's exploration of the similarities between Christian and Buddhist teaching and practice. In anticipation of his discussion of the significance of the Christian eucharist (Lord's supper), he explains the Buddhist practice of looking deeply into food.

Mindful eating is an important practice. It nourishes awareness in us. Children are very capable of practicing with us. In Buddhist monasteries, we eat our meals in silence to make it easier to give our full attention to the food and to the other members of the community who are present. And we chew each morsel thoroughly, at least thirty times, to help us be truly in touch with it. Eating this way is very good for digestion.

Before every meal, a monk or a nun recites the Five Contemplations: "This food is the gift of the whole universe—the earth, the sky and much hard work. May we live in a way that is worthy of this food. May we transform our unskillful states of mind, especially that of greed. May we eat only foods that nourish us and prevent illness. May we accept this food for the realization of the way of understanding and love."

Then we look at the food deeply, in a way that allows it to become real. Contemplating our food before eating in mindfulness can be a real source of happiness. Every time I hold a bowl of rice, I know how fortunate I am. I know that forty thousand children die every day because of the lack of food and that many people are lonely, without friends or family. I visualize them and feel deep compassion. You don't need to be in a monastery to practice this. You can practice at home at your dinner table. Eating mindfully is a wonderful way to nourish compassion, and it encourages us to do something to help those who are hungry and lonely. We needn't be afraid of eating without having the TV, radio, newspaper or a complicated conversation to distract us. In fact, it is wonderful and joyful to be completely present with our food.[13]

REFLECT AND ACT

By yourself, or in cooperation with others, engage in the following reflection and action exercises. Try to do one exercise each day for a week. If one activity is particularly meaningful, stay with it for a longer period of time. Also feel free to create exercises of your own as you are inspired by the life and witness of Thich Nhat Hanh.

1. Thây Nhat Hanh recommends taking time for mindful breathing and smiling throughout the day. Here is a short poem that you can memorize and recite as often as you think of it. Remember to smile and breathe!

   Breathing in, I calm my body.
   Breathing out, I smile.
   Dwelling in the present moment
   I know this is a wonderful moment.[14]

2. Reflect on the meaning of true happiness and on the conditions that seem necessary to make happiness possible. If those conditions ceased to exist, would happiness disappear as well? Consider how Nhat Hanh's understanding of being happy in the present moment offers a new way of seeking happiness.

3. Read a book by someone who is reflecting deeply on his or her involvement in the Vietnam War. For example, in his book *In Retrospect: The Tragedy and Lessons of Vietnam* (New York: Vintage, 1996), former Secretary of Defense Robert McNamara questions the wisdom of the United States' involvement in the war. Similarly, in *My Father, My Son* (1986) former Chief of Naval Operations Admiral Elmo Zumwalt writes of his son's death from cancer as a direct result of the Admiral's decision to use Agent Orange so close to U.S. military troops. Reflect on the spiritual dimension of their experiences. How has time and the wisdom of maturity created a new perspective on the Vietnam War?

4. Engage in walking meditation, either alone or with companions. Breathe normally, but take mindful steps on the earth. Be aware of each breath and step and keep a slight smile on your lips. Be attentive to your connection with the Earth and be strengthened by her power. (For more guidance on this powerful practice, see Thich Nhat Hanh's *The Long Road Turns to Joy*.)

5. Reflect on Nhat Hanh's poem "Please Call Me by My True Names." What are the difficulties and dangers of seeing oneself as both the twelve-year-old girl and the sea pirate who raped her? How is one's understanding transformed when viewing oneself as both the hungry child in Uganda and the arms merchant?

6. Think back to your childhood and search your memory for a spiritual or mystical moment like the one experienced by Nhat Hanh when he was searching for the hermit. Recall as many details as you can, such as where it took place, what sights and sounds there were, who else was present, how it made you feel, and whether or not you told anyone about it and how they responded. Become like a child and represent

your spiritual moment artistically, through drawing, painting, singing, or dancing. How did you know that this moment was special? What impact did it have on your future spiritual development?

7. Sit down and talk with a refugee. This person could be a recent immigrant or one of the "displaced persons" who left Europe during World War II. Let him or her tell the story and share the feelings about leaving home to begin a new life in a foreign country. Afterward, meditate on what he or she has told you, imagining yourself to be one with him or her. Are you able to put yourself in her place? Can you empathize with his feelings? What can you learn from this exercise?

8. Choose one country or region of the world where violent conflict rages today. Read the newspaper and scan the Internet to learn as much as you can about the issues and arguments of both sides. Assuming a spirit of complete neutrality, brainstorm ways in which peace can be found without designating one side "right" and the other side "wrong." How could each side come to really understand the pain of their so-called enemy?

9. As you sit down to eat one meal, pause for several minutes to look deeply into your food. Can you see the soil, sky, and water that nurtured it, and the hands that tended and harvested it? Can you be mindful of those who are hungry on this day? In light of this awareness, what would be an appropriate way to show gratitude for what you are receiving to eat?

10. Meditate for several minutes on the suffering of someone other than yourself. This person could be someone you know well or an unknown victim of violence or poverty. Imagine yourself becoming one with that person, feeling the pain, frustration, and hopelessness he or she feels. Do you also detect joy amid the sorrow? What is one thing that your sense of compassion and understanding is leading you to do to alleviate the suffering of this other?

11. Research the plight of refugees around the world. What are they fleeing in their country of origin? Where are they seeking to go, and what do they hope to find there? What are the

government leaders saying about their departure? Like Nhat Hanh, do not focus on which side is "right," but rather look deeply into the suffering experienced by those on both sides.

For Further Reading

Ingram, Catherine. "Thich Nhat Hanh." In *In the Footsteps of Gandhi: Conversations with Spiritual Social Activists.* Berkeley: Parallax Press, 1990.

Nhat Hanh, Thich. *Being Peace.* Berkeley: Parallax Press, 1987.

——. *The Sun My Heart.* Berkeley: Parallax Press, 1988.

——. *Touching Peace: Practicing the Art of Mindful Living.* Berkeley: Parallax Press, 1992.

——. *Living Buddha, Living Christ.* New York: Riverhead Books, 1995.

——. *Cultivating the Mind of Love:The Practice of Looking Deeply in the Mahayana Buddhist Tradition.* Berkeley: Parallax Press, 1996.

——. *The Long Road Turns to Joy: A Guide to Walking Meditation.* Berkeley: Parallax Press, 1996.

——. *Interbeing: Fourteen Guidelines for Engaged Buddhism.* Edited by Fred Eppsteiner. 3d ed. Berkeley: Parallax Press, 1998.

Notes

[1] Thich Nhat Hanh, *Cultivating the Mind of Love: The Practice of Looking Deeply in the Mahayana Buddhist Tradition* (Berkeley: Parallax, 1996), 8–9.

[2] Thich Nhat Hanh, *Being Peace* (Berkeley: Parallax, 1987), 85–88.

[3] Catherine Ingram, "Thich Nhat Hanh," in *In the Footsteps of Gandhi: Conversations with Spiritual Social Activists* (Berkeley: Parallax, 1990), 90; and Thich Nhat Hanh, *The Sun My Heart* (Berkeley: Parallax, 1988), 123–24.

[4] Nhat Hanh, *Being Peace,* 37.

[5] Thich Nhat Hanh, *Interbeing: Fourteen Guidelines for Engaged Buddhism,* ed. Fred Eppsteiner, 3d ed. (Berkeley: Parallax, 1998), 65.

[6] Thich Nhat Hanh, *Living Buddha, Living Christ* (New York: Riverhead Books, 1995), 118–19.

[7] Ingram, 94.

[8] Ibid., 89.

[9] Nhat Hanh, *Being Peace,* 13–15.

[10] Nhat Hanh, *Cultivating the Mind of Love,* 69.

[11] *Being Peace,* 62–64.

[12] Thich Nhat Hanh, *Touching Peace: Practicing the Art of Mindfulness* (Berkeley: Parallax, 1992), 23–25.

[13] Nhat Hanh, *Living Budda, Living Christ,* 27–28.

[14] Nhat Hanh, *Being Peace,* 5.

Chapter Six

Rigoberta Menchú

Champion of Indian Rights in Guatemala

PREPARE TO MEDITATE

Recall a story of serious hardship. Perhaps it is a story told to you by a family member or friend or something you read in a newspaper or novel. Now imagine that you yourself are undergoing this hardship. What do you feel? Who or what supports you in your trial? What spiritual resources are available to you? Conclude your meditation by praying for those who suffer and thanking God for those things that sustain during times of trial.

HEAR THE STORIES

Although she stands barely five feet tall, Rigoberta Menchú expresses the confidence and inner strength of a person twice her height. Her joyful smile and hopeful demeanor hide the intense pain she has suffered in her short lifetime. Her story recounts the unspeakable suffering that human beings are capable of inflicting on one another, as well as the incredible ability of the human spirit to carry on with courage and hope in the face of such deep pain.

Menchú is a Quiché Indian from Guatemala, one of the numerous indigenous peoples whose histories reach back for centuries in the Americas. She came into this world in 1959, the sixth of nine children born to Juana Tum and Vicente Menchú. She was born in Chimel, a village near San Miguel de Uspantan, the capital of the province of El Quiché, in the northern, mountainous region of Guatemala.

The history of the Quiché Indians goes back to the ancient Mayans, whose cultural and artistic endeavors continue to astound people even today. They have a particularly rich religious heritage, a unique blend of traditional and more contemporary religious rites and teachings. Their traditional religion, passed down to them through generations of ancestors, combines a deep love for the natural world and devotion to the Earth in gratitude for all she provides. The newer religious strain is that of Roman Catholicism, brought to them by Spanish missionaries in the 1500s. They celebrate Catholic rites, such as baptism and communion, in addition to their traditional ceremonies. Because the Quiché live so close to nature, they view all of life as worship, and, consequently, they remain in a constant state of prayer. They offer prayers upon rising early in the morning, asking God to bless their new day. Women pray when lighting the wood for the fire in gratitude for the way in which it will provide food for the entire family. Likewise, men remove their hats (all Quiché wear hats to protect them from the strong rays of the sun) and talk to the sun before beginning their work in the morning. This prayerful attitude is part of every daily activity.

When Rigoberta was a baby, her parents tried to establish a home in the town of Chimel, but they were chased away by *ladinos*, people of mixed Spaniard and Indian ancestry who believe themselves to be superior in every way to the native Indians. As a result of this pervasive prejudice, the Quiché Indians settled in the mountains, where conditions are rugged and farming difficult. Each year they were able to spend only four months at their home in the mountains before the food ran out. There they ate plants that grew wild, beans they had planted, and tortillas made from the maize they grew.

The community has elaborate sacred ceremonies to celebrate both the sowing and the harvesting of beans and maize. Before planting the seeds, the members of the community ask the Earth for permission to cultivate her. All the villagers say prayers and light candles, then the seeds that are to be sown are brought before the assembled community. Two or three of the largest corn seeds or beans are chosen for the ceremony. They are placed in the center of a ring of four candles, representing earth, water, animals, and human beings. Prayers are offered for all those things that contribute to making the food grow: the sun, moon, earth, water, and animals. Every family also makes a vow not to waste any of the food that is produced. (In fact, the Quiché use every part of the corn plant, including the cob, to make food for the animals and the leaves for wrapping *tamales.*) The next day, all the families rejoice as they sow their seeds. Later, on harvest day, the beans and maize are not gathered up until after the community joins together in a ceremony thanking the Earth and God for feeding them.[1]

The Roman Catholic Church was also quite active in the region where the Menchús lived. Because of her bright spirit and willingness to learn, Rigoberta was chosen as a catechist at the age of twelve. Since the priest only visited their village every three months, she was responsible for teaching Catholic doctrine to the people. The priest left behind books for her to study, but since she could not read Spanish, she had to teach completely from memory. She taught people to pray the Rosary, offered prayers on behalf of the sick and the dying, recited Catholic prayers in Latin, collected money to buy things the community needed, sang Catholic songs, and studied biblical texts in small groups, leading people in a discussion of how to live the Christian life. Her work as a catechist laid the foundation for Menchú's later activism, by both providing a biblical basis for her work and preparing her to organize large groups of people.

When the crops ran out, the Quiché traveled across rough terrain to the *fincas,* the coastal plantations, where they worked for meager wages picking coffee or cotton for the wealthy landowners. Because so many Indians seek work in the *fincas,* the workers are regularly mistreated, given little to eat, and forced to sleep three hundred or more in a communal house on the plantation property. Menchú remembers first beginning to work on the coffee plantations at the age of eight, then picking cotton at ten. The workday began at three o'clock in the morning and continued late into the afternoon as workers labored in the hot sun. Two of Menchú's brothers died working on the *finca.* Her eldest brother, Filipe, died before she was born; he was poisoned by pesticides. She was eight when her youngest brother

Nicolás died from malnutrition at the age of two, his small stomach distended from hunger.

The death that made the strongest impression on her, however, was that of her friend Maria, when Menchú was thirteen years old. Maria also died from pesticide poisoning when the owners were spraying the cotton. Every day Menchú tried to cope with her grief over the death of this vibrant young woman. She watched as her mother bravely carried on despite her obvious grief over the death of her sons and her inability to provide a better life for her children. Menchú grew increasingly angry and depressed, wondering what life would be like for her when she grew up. Could she bear having to live like this until she grew old? Hoping to change her life and provide more income for her family, Menchú left the *fincas* at age thirteen to work as a maid in Guatemala City. The rich *ladinos* for whom she worked paid her little, worked her very hard, and treated their fat dog better than they treated her. She left after four months. Upon returning to her family she discovered that her father had been taken to prison.

By now it was the 1970s. Throughout that decade and into the 1980s as well, Guatemala's government was headed by presidents who cracked down on "subversives" and "terrorists" they deemed a threat to the state. Vicente Menchú, a leader in the Indian movement to overcome oppression, was a constant target of government repression. His leadership began innocently enough: the rich landowners tried again and again to evict the Indians from their land in the mountains, wanting to appropriate it for themselves. On several occasions, the Quiché communities were violently forced from their homes, their possessions looted or destroyed, their animals killed. Although unable to read or write, Vicente mediated negotiations between the Indians and the *ladinos*. When the *ladinos* failed to honor the agreement allowing the Indians to remain on their land, the Indians fought back with the only weapons they had—sticks, stones, hot water, chili, and salt.

Menchú's father was in prison for fourteen months. During that year, she continually traveled between Guatemala City and her mountain village attempting to secure the legal assistance the family needed to get him released. After his release, he was kidnapped, tortured, and left for dead on the side of the road—a message to the Indian community to stop their resistance. He needed nine months of convalescence to recover from his injuries, but emerged stronger and more determined than ever to mobilize the people. Although only a teenager, Menchú traveled everywhere with her father from then on, learning the little bit of Spanish she needed to carry on negotiations and meeting with government leaders in the capital city.

Drawing on her experience as a catechist, Menchú began to travel from village to village, teaching people the principles from the Bible that supported the peasants' right to live free from tyranny and danger. Her study of the Bible convinced her that certain Catholic priests were wrong in teaching the people that God wanted them to be submissive to the government in preparation for a heavenly reward in the life to come. She led the people in learning from the example of biblical people who resisted oppression in the name of God. Men identified with Moses, who led the Israelites out of the hands of the Egyptian oppressors. Women found courage in the example of Judith, who did not stop fighting the king until she had cut off his head. Children were inspired by the story of the shepherd boy David, who, despite all odds, slew the mighty Goliath. From these stories they could see that what they were now suffering had also been suffered by their ancestors! Like their biblical ancestors, they too could overcome and be victorious. After all, the Bible is very clear, Menchú says, that God gives everyone the right to eat. It is not God but greedy people who impose suffering on others. Thus, like their biblical counterparts, they have the responsibility to use any means, including violence, to bring an end to oppression.[2]

Although the people were ready to use violence if necessary, very often their biblical training had the opposite effect, compelling them to seek nonviolent ways to resolve conflict. Menchú tells of how the members of her village prepared themselves in case they were attacked by government soldiers. They rebuilt their homes closer to one another and placed lookouts at each of the four corners of the village. They made an evacuation plan and set up an alternate camp high in the mountains. They created traps around the perimeter of the village and collected as many weapons as possible, using their vast knowledge of the natural world. They vowed that they would not allow even one villager to be kidnapped.

Their courage was tested for the first time when their look-out announced that soldiers were coming. The villagers retreated to the mountains. Unable to find anyone in town, the soldiers pillaged the Indians' homes and killed their animals. Rather than sit around and wait, the villagers decided to ambush the army when it traveled along the mountain pass. A young woman volunteered to distract the soldiers. She talked with a few of the soldiers, who asked her where the people in the village had gone. She successfully detained one soldier long enough that he got separated from the others. This gave the villagers their opportunity to capture him. Tricking him into thinking that they were holding a gun to his head, they got him to drop his weapons—a pistol, a rifle, several rounds of ammunition, and grenades. Menchú remembers finding this whole incident quite funny: Here they were, pointing weapons that they did not even know how to use at a frightened government soldier!

They joyously took him back to their village, but they did nothing to harm him in any way. They sat him down in a chair and, one by one, members of the community came in to tell him why the army should give up their repression of the peasants. This soldier, an Indian from a different ethnic group, was told about the suffering of the people, about their God-given right to occupy the land they had cultivated, and about the rich people's oppression of the Indians and the poor. Three hours after his capture, the Indian solider left the village, charged with the task of bringing this message to his fellow soldiers. Sadly, the soldier was killed as a deserter upon his return to his company. Nevertheless, the army stayed away from the village for a very long time, obviously frightened by the resourcefulness and resolve of the Quiché people.[3]

The Menchú family's involvement in the peasant movement also resulted in tremendous personal tragedy. In 1979, Menchú's youngest living brother, Patrocinio, was kidnapped, tortured, and burned alive in front of his family and members of his village. Then on January 31, 1980, her father died during a protest in Guatemala City. A group of Indians marched on the capital, took over radio stations, and occupied the Spanish Embassy. The entire group was killed by the army. A few months later, Menchú's mother was also kidnapped, tortured, and left to die on a hilltop, her body eaten by wild animals.

These terrible occurrences brought about a change in the people of Guatemala. Now people from all walks of life—the poor, the middle-class, and professionals—began to speak out against the government. Many risked their lives just by attending the funerals of those who died in the raid on the Spanish Embassy. In 1981, the 31 January Popular Front was formed so that the brave sacrifice of these Indians would not be forgotten. Likewise, a religious organization was set up in the name of Menchú's father—the Vicente Menchú Revolutionary Christians. He was remembered as a man who never lost his faith despite the dire circumstances that he constantly faced.

As of 1981, Menchú was in hiding and self-imposed exile in Mexico. By this time she was on the verge of losing hope. Barely twenty-three years old, she had experienced more suffering than most undergo in a lifetime. Fortuitously, she ran into one of her younger sisters, also active in organizing the people, also in hiding. Her twelve-year-old sister reminded Menchú that they were revolutionary women who must not give up hope. "What has happened is a sign of victory," she said. "We have to fight without measuring our suffering or what we experience or thinking about the monstrous things we must bear in life." At the same time, Menchú grew quite ill, having developed a serious ulcer. While she was sleeping, her parents came to her in a dream and told her, "You are a woman. That's enough of that!" She says her body was instantly healed, and her spirit was filled with joy. The love and support of her family gave her the strength to continue the work to which she had been called.[4]

From her new home base in Mexico, Menchú gave her energies to helping organize rebel Indians living in the Guatemalan mountains. Soon after, she was invited to speak to the United Nations about the plight of indigenous peoples. She became a frequent presence in the halls of the United Nations, as she and a small group of Guatemalans-in-exile called attention to human rights violations in their native land. Through her experience she learned much about the political workings of government, but was sorely disappointed by the apathy of politicians. While U. N. officials listened patiently to the heart-wrenching stories of the refugees, very little seemed to move them to action. She also embarked on a tour of the United States and Europe, where she told her story to many sympathetic hearers. Empowered by her efforts, Menchú returned to Guatemala City in 1988, where she was immediately arrested. The government soon released her, however, under intense pressure from U. N. leaders. Because of the danger, she was unable to make Guatemala her permanent home until 1993. By this time, she had married her husband Angel Francisco Canil, and the couple had one son.

Menchú won the Nobel Peace Prize in 1992. Her nomination met with strong disapproval from the Guatemalan government, which views her as the instigator of the armed resistance of the peasants. Nevertheless, the prize has brought worldwide attention to the plight of indigenous peoples in Guatemala and other parts of Central America. She used the prize money to set up a foundation that bears her name. The organization has two goals: to carry out a peace mission in honor of all those who have died in the struggle in Central America and to encourage new forms of economic development that take account of the needs and rights of indigenous peoples.

Menchú's international fame has also brought greater scrutiny to the book that bears her name, *I, Rigoberta Menchú.* The book contains the interviews journalist Elisabeth Burgos-Debray carried out with Menchú in the early 1980s. A challenge is mounted by anthropologist David Stoll who, in his book *Rigoberta Menchú and the Story of All Poor Guatemalans* (Boulder, Colo.: Westview Press), believes that Burgos-Debray's book misrepresents the Guatemalan situation when it describes a clear-cut struggle between the evil national army and the righteous guerrillas and peasants. In his interviews with the indigenous peoples, he discovered that the Indians were actually caught in between the army and the guerrillas, both of whom could be quite ruthless. While he does not doubt Menchú's account of the suffering of the Quiché people, he does believe that the book was written primarily as a propaganda tool of international human rights leaders who wanted to swing the balance of power in the direction of the guerrillas. The book was indeed quite successful in doing this, though Stoll questions the truth of the accounts Menchú supposedly offers in that book.[5]

However flawed the reporting of her story might be, the fact remains that the world has been introduced to a young woman, Rigoberta Menchú, whose love for the land and her people, coupled with a strong desire to know and do the will of God, compels her to act with courage on behalf of the land and the people in the name of God.

READ THE WORDS

As you read the works that follow, ask yourself these questions: What are some ways in which Menchú's words connect to her life story? How do they nurture my spiritual life and/or inspire me to engage in acts of social justice?

READING ONE:

The Popol Vuh, *or "Council Book," is the ancient sacred text of the Quiché Indians. It chronicles the adventures of the gods and describes their reverence for all of nature, cosmic and physical. The story is told of how the gods, here named Bearer, Begetter, Maker, Modeler, and Sovereign Plumed Serpent, attempt three times to create human beings but fail each time because they do not have the right ingredients. On the fourth attempt, however, they are successful because they learn of the existence of white and yellow corn, the two essential elements of the Indian people. From corn they create the four primordial humans from whom all Indians are descended.*

And here is the beginning of the conception of humans, and of the search for the ingredients of the human body. So they spoke, the Bearer, Begetter, the Makers, Modelers named Sovereign Plumed Serpent:

"The dawn has approached, preparations have been made, and morning has come for the provider, nurturer, born in the light, begotten in the light. Morning has come for humankind, for the people of the face of the earth," they said. It all came together as they went on thinking in the darkness, in the night, as they searched and sifted, they thought and they wondered.

And here their thoughts came out in clear light. They sought and discovered what was needed for human flesh. It was only a short while before the sun, moon and stars were to appear above the Makers and Modelers. Split Place, Bitter Water Place is the name: the yellow corn, white corn came from there. ["Split Place" is the town labeled on maps as Zacualpa.]

And these are the names of the animals who brought the food: fox, coyote, parrot, crow. There were four animals who brought the news of the ears of yellow corn and white corn. They were coming from over there at Split Place, they showed the way to the split.

And this was when they found the staple foods.

And these were the ingredients for the flesh of the human work, the human design, and the water was for the blood. It became human blood, and corn was also used by the Bearer, Begetter...

And then the yellow corn and white corn were ground, and Xmucane [the divine midwife who is prior to all birth] did the grinding nine times. Food was used, along with the water she rinsed her hands with, for the creation of grease; it became human fat when it was worked by the Bearer, Begetter, Sovereign Plumed Servant, as they are called.

After that, they put it into words:

the making, the modeling of our first mother-father,
with yellow corn, white corn alone for the flesh,
food alone for the human legs and arms,
for our first fathers, the four human works.

It was staples alone that made up their flesh.[6]

READING TWO:

In 1982, Menchú spent one week in Paris telling her life story to author Elisabeth Burgos-Debray. Burgos-Debray taped the interviews and subsequently put Menchú's words down on paper to create the book I, Rigoberta Menchú. *Originally published in Spanish, it has been translated into twelve languages. The following two readings are excerpts from that book. In this first selection, Menchú describes the importance of prayer in the Quiché Indian community.*

The prayers and ceremonies are for the whole community. We pray to our ancestors, reciting their prayers which have been known to us for a long time—a very, very long time. We evoke the representatives of the animal world; we say the names of dogs. We say the names of the earth, the God of the earth, and the God of water. Then we say the name of the heart of the sky—the Sun. Our grandfathers say we must ask the sun to shine on all its children: the trees, animals, water, man. We ask it to shine on our enemies...

A prayer is made up of all this. We make a definite plea to the earth. We say: "Mother Earth, you who gives us food, whose children we are and on whom we depend, please make this produce you give us flourish and make our children and our animals grow...," and others' things as well. Or we say: "We make our vows for ten days so that you concede us permission, your permission, Mother Earth, who are sacred, to feed us and give our children what they need. We do not abuse you, we only beg your permission, you who are part of the natural world and part of the family of our parents and our grandparents." This means we believe, for instance, that the sun is our grandfather, that he is a member of our family. "We respect you and love you and ask that you love us as we love you."—those prayers are specially for the earth.

For the sun we say: "Heart of the sky, you are our father, we ask you to give your warmth and light to our animals, our maize, our beans, our plants, so that they may grow and our children may eat." We evoke the colour of the sun, and this has a special importance for us because this is how we want our children to live—like a light which shines, which shines with generosity. It means a warm heart and it means strength, life-giving strength. So when we evoke the colour of the sun, it's like evoking all the elements which go to make up our life. The sun, as the channel to the one God, receives the plea from his children that they should never violate the rights of all the other beings which surround them. This is how we renew our prayer which says that men, the children of the one God, must respect the life of the trees, the birds, the animals around us.[7]

READING THREE:

With these words Menchú tells of the encouragement and inspiration she has received from the Bible, particularly the life and witness of Christ.

I am a Christian and I participate in this struggle as a Christian. For me, as a Christian, there is one important thing. That is the life of Christ. Throughout his life Christ was humble. History tells us he was born in a little hut. He was persecuted and had to form a band of men so that his seed would not disappear. They were his disciples, his apostles. In those days, there was no other way of defending himself or Christ would have used it against his oppressors, against his enemies. He even gave his life. But Christ did not die, because generations and generations have followed him. And that's exactly what we understood when our first catechists fell. They're dead but our people keep their memory alive through our struggle against the government, against an enemy who oppresses us. We don't need very much advice, or theories, or documents: life has been our teacher...

For us the Bible is our main weapon. It has shown us the way. Perhaps those who call themselves Christians but are really only Christians in theory, won't understand why we give the Bible the meaning we do. But that's because they haven't lived as we have. And also perhaps because they can't analyse it. I can assure you that any one of my community, even though he's illiterate and has to have it read to him and translated into his language, can learn many lessons from it, because he has no difficulty understanding what reality is and what the difference is between the paradise up above, in Heaven, and the reality of our people here on Earth. We do this because we feel it is the duty of Christians to create the kingdom of God on Earth among our brothers. This kingdom will exist only when we all have enough to eat, when our children, brothers, parents don't have to die from hunger and malnutrition. That will be the "Glory," a Kingdom for we who have never known it.[8]

READING FOUR:

In the 1990s, Menchú set out to update her story and to resolve some of the misunderstandings created by her first book. The result was Crossing Borders, *published in 1998. The following passage tells of the racist attitudes she confronts regularly in her travels.*

There is something quite important that people don't know. I always travel like any other citizen of the world, squat and dark-skinned as I have always been. I will always have the face of a poor woman, my Mayan face, my indigenous face. At official ceremonies when I am received by a king or a head of state,

I am the winner of the Nobel Peace Prize. When there is a *coup d'état* or some other conflict, and my presence is requested, I am the winner of the Nobel Peace Prize. Yet when I cross borders, it's another story. Customs and immigration officials act impatiently. They take my things out one by one, even my underclothes. They are often very offensive and racist.

After they have finished going through my things, taking out my *huipils* [the traditional Indian dress for women], and making me pack my case again, I always teach them a little awareness. You need humanity wherever you are. "The world should be a fairer place," I tell them, "it should be more humane, less aggressive and less racist." I start to give them a talk.

When my case is finally packed again, I take out my identity papers and say, "Look, I'm a humble winner of the Nobel Peace Prize, and the humble president of a Foundation devoted to peace studies, civic responsibility and teaching the world about the profound value of ancient indigenous cultures."

They are of course very surprised. I know they will never forget me. They will probably be among the most avid readers of this book. So everything serves some purpose. I believe that the dignity of the people of Guatemala, their strength, their struggles and their creativity, are part of life. No one can dislodge us from here, not by violence, war or hatred. Let us hope this will always be so. I dream of living in a Guatemala at peace. Some day.[9]

READING FIVE:
Here Menchú offers her hope that religious differences can be a cause for celebration and mutual understanding, rather than a source of conflict and hatred.

I am deeply religious, yet I also believe in nature. I believe in life and peoples. I believe in people's faith and their communion. I believe in the life experiences and faith of the early Christians, above all because they believed in sharing things. I believe we human beings must fight for creation; and by this I mean all of the planet's living things.

I also believe firmly that people need to believe. I have always maintained that the faith of a person or a people is sacred and private. It cannot be bought or sold. It has no price. A people's religion and their religious sensibility must be respected. We Mayans have retained the essence of our faith. It must be allowed to flourish, and we must have the right to proclaim it. If the religions of the Mayans, and the Incas and the Aztecs lack full recognition and a measure of institutionalisation, then we must fight for these things too.

A people's religious sensibility is based on daily practice and a humble attitude to life. If religion is not understood in this sense, it becomes a commodity or an obstacle to peaceful coexistence. It risks becoming a weapon of colonialism, of discord and racism, of dictatorship and war. Religious sensibility is ingrained in a people, throughout their history and down the generations. It lies behind the laws that have governed the daily life of our civilisations for thousands of years...

The challenge for the future lies in understanding and accepting diversity. We must prevent religious conflicts from concealing fundamental economic problems. The rich and powerful can always use religion to cover up injustices and, worse still, religion can be used as one of the main planks of impunity...

We still have to find a way of preventing instruments of religion from becoming instruments of war. Whenever the indigenous peoples of the continent reaffirm their own religion, governments often say that they are attacking national unity. Yet what the people really want is to make governments understand that both diversity and national unity must be based on mutual respect. Our contradictions do not stem from religion, but from a lack of mutual respect and of intercultural coexistence.[10]

Reflect and Act

By yourself, or in cooperation with others, engage in the following reflection and action exercises. Try to do one exercise each day for a week. If one activity is particularly meaningful, stay with it for a longer period of time. Also feel free to create exercises of your own as you are inspired by the life and witness of Rigoberta Menchú.

1. Make a list of the regular activities you participate in each day, such as going out to get the newspaper, making coffee, washing dishes, driving to work, picking up the children after

school, etc. Recognize the sacredness of these actions by developing a short prayer to accompany each one: "God, guide me that I might read this newspaper with insight and compassion" or "May these clean dishes be a symbol of pure minds and hearts." Let these short prayers bring new meaning to and appreciation for the daily activities of your life.

2. Amnesty International USA is a human rights organization that keeps track of prisoners of conscience throughout the world and brings to light the human rights violations of governments. Contact AIUSA at 322 Eighth Avenue, New York City, NY 10001, phone 212-807-8400, fax 212-627-1451 or at their Internet address http://www.amnesty.org. Read the stories of political and religious prisoners of conscience and consider joining a letter-writing campaign to secure their release.

3. Reflect on the various rituals that are important in your life. Think not just of religious rites, but of personal, family, and community events that occur with some regularity and carry certain meaning, for example, a daily walk, yearly Thanksgiving dinner, or summer concerts in the park. What makes these rituals so special? What would you lose if one or all of these rituals were missing from your life? What other rituals would you like to engage in on a more regular basis? Choose one and determine how to do this.

4. Menchú says that the Bible is her "main weapon" in the struggle for freedom. Referring to the peasants' willingness to use violence against their oppressors, she says that other Christians "won't understand why we give the Bible the meaning we do. But that's because they haven't lived as we have." Recalling that Menchú taught the Bible from memory, consider what arguments you can develop for and against the use of violence based on your knowledge of the Bible. What is your understanding of what God wants for people and the world?

5. Meditate about the differences between rich and poor, both as Menchú describes them and as you experience them in the world. What are your prejudices about each of these groups? Use this as an opportunity to reflect on the rights

and responsibilities of people who live at different socio-economic levels of society. What are *your* rights and responsibilities?

6. Liberation theology stresses God's preference for the poor and oppressed and challenges Christians to seek to overcome oppressive forces in the world. Liberation theology is represented by many forms, including black theology, feminist theology, and Latin American liberation theology. Read portions of works by liberation theologians, such as James Cone, *Black Theology and Black Power;* Rosemary Radford Ruether, *Sexism and God-Talk;* Mary Daly, *The Church and the Second Sex;* or Gustavo Gutierrez, *A Theology of Liberation.* Other books may be found by searching for "liberation theology" on the library computer. How do these writers challenge your concepts of God and the purpose of religion?

7. Decide to view all of nature—the sun and moon; plants, animals, and insects; and the changes in weather—as sacred for one day. In what ways do you live your life disconnected from the natural world? Imagine some part of nature—a favorite tree, an animal, the wind—speaking to you. What would it say?

8. Remember a time when you had to work together with someone you would not normally associate with in order to accomplish a common goal. Try to recall as many details about that time as you possibly can. What understandings did the two of you reach? What conflicts were resolved or left unresolved? What did you learn through that experience?

9. Meditate on the life of Christ. Do this by reflecting on how the example of Christ has inspired you; by contemplating one teaching, miracle, or other story from the gospels; or by following a series of events in the life of Christ, such as his passion and death. Visualize yourself in the scene with Christ. What does he say and do that speaks to your situation in life? How does he challenge you to live?

10. Bring to mind someone who gave you hope during a time when you were in despair. Write about this experience, make a drawing, work with clay, create a series of arm movements and dance steps, or compose a poem or song to express the

impact this person had on you. Another option is to develop before and after representations—how things were before this person influenced you and how you felt after your encounter with him or her.

11. Menchú not only dedicates her life's work to the struggle for freedom in Guatemala but also is willing to give up her life, if necessary. To what cause or belief are you willing to give your life's work? Would you also be willing to give up your life for that same cause or belief? Why or why not? What are the similarities and differences between your situation and Menchú's?

FOR FURTHER READING

Graham, Judith, ed. "Rigoberta Menchú." In *Current Biography Yearbook 1993*. New York: Wilson Company, 1993.

Menchú, Rigoberta. *I, Rigoberta Menchú: An Indian Woman in Guatamala*. Edited and introduced by Elisabeth Burgos-Debray. Translated by Ann Wright. London, New York: Verso, 1984.

——. *Crossing Borders*. Translated and edited by Ann Wright. London, New York: Verso, 1998.

Popol Vuh: The Mayan Book of the Dawn of Life. Translated by Dennis Tedlock. New York: Touchstone, 1986.

Notes

[1] Rigoberta Menchú, *I, Rigoberta Menchú*, ed. Elisabeth Burgos-Debray, trans. Ann Wright (London, New York: Verso 1984), 52–55.

[2] Ibid., 131–32.

[3] Ibid., 135–39.

[4] Ibid., 236–37.

[5] David Stoll, *Rigoberta Menchú and the Story of All Poor Guatemalans* (Boulder, Colo.: Westview, 1999), viii–xv.

[6] *Popol Vuh: The Mayan Book of the Dawn of Life,* trans. Dennis Tedlock (New York: Touchstone, 1986), 145–46.

[7] Menchú, *I, Rigoberta Menchú*, 57–58.

[8] Ibid., 132–33, 134.

[9] Rigoberta Menchú, *Crossing Borders*, trans. and ed. Ann Wright (London, New York: Verso, 1998), 21.

[10] Ibid., 216–17.

Chapter Seven

Vine Deloria, Jr.

Speaking Out for Native American Self-determination

Prepare to Meditate

Sitting in a quiet place, perhaps indoors with a candle or outdoors beneath a tree, meditate on some aspect of your spiritual heritage. Choose a doctrine that you learned, a ritual that you found meaningful, a person who was influential, a book that moved you to reflect and/or act, or a work of art that touched your heart. (Feel free to meditate on the same aspect every time you participate in this exercise, or choose a different one each time.) Reflect on how these spiritual inheritances gave meaning to your religious experience and gave shape to your maturing self.

Hear the Stories

The Lakota[1] tell the story of how Taku Wakan, the Great Spirit, took clay from the earth and fashioned it into the first Indian. The story begins with the affirmation that Taku Wakan absolutely loved the beauty of the physical Earth and all the animals that inhabited it. He determined, however, to make one more creature, one far superior to animals and one who would be the master of all. Many times he formed the creature out of clay with his hands and held it over the fire to harden the form and give it color, but each time he was disappointed with the outcome. Sometimes the figure would turn out a pale, ashy color;

other times it would become dark brown or black from remaining in the fire too long. With patience he toiled on.

Then one day, Taku Wakan was pleased to produce the perfect form, beautiful in color and shape. He made a second one as well, so that they could reproduce and fill the land. He gently breathed into them the breath of life and gave them the name "Lakota." Stretching out his arm and pointing to the beautiful lands, he gave them to the Lakota for their home. These lands are known today as the Americas.

Although he believed his other creations to be inferior to the Lakota, Taku Wakan did not discard them but breathed the breath of life into them as well. He put them in lands of their own and separated them from the Lakota by placing great waters between them. This is how, the Lakota say, God formed the many nations of the earth, giving to each their own land in which to live. But, the legend continues, among all the peoples of the earth, the Lakota have been God's favorite from the beginning of time.[2]

This legend stands in the tradition of similar creation stories told by religious groups throughout the world, all of which affirm their own specialness in the eyes of God. Likewise, it highlights the spiritual aspect of Indian life and the deep connection native peoples have with one another, the Great Spirit, and the land that was given to them. This story also serves as a backdrop for the life and work of Vine Deloria, Jr., a Yankton Sioux writer, lawyer, and Indian activist. He has sought to explain to white folk the deeper significance of the Indians' relationship to the land and to protect—through writing, protests, and legal action—the Indians' rights to live on the land on which they lived peacefully until they were displaced by whites.

Vine Deloria, Jr., was born into a distinguished Sioux family in 1933. His great-grandfather was a well-known tribal medicine man; his grandfather, Philip, was a missionary priest of the Episcopal Church; his aunt Ella was an ethnographer who wrote about Indian life and language; and his father, Vine, Sr., was also an Episcopal priest and the first American Indian to be named to a national executive position in that denomination.

The young Deloria grew up on the Pine Ridge Indian Reservation in South Dakota. From early on, he remembers a world hostile to Native American people and their ways. Throughout South Dakota, for instance, signs reading "No Dogs and No Indians Allowed" were displayed prominently for all to see. Oklahoma Indians were so degraded that many had come truly to believe that they were inferior to whites. Indians in Washington State endured the increasing curtailment of fishing rights that had been guaranteed by six treaties with the U.S. government. In fact, numerous "fish-ins" occurred in the early 1970s as activists from all over the country traveled to the Pacific Northwest to show their support for Native American rights.[3]

As a child, Deloria often heard the ancient stories of his people mixed together with the teachings of Christianity. He learned very early that white folk and red folk had very different ways of looking at the world: the whites put all their faith in science, technology, and rational explanations while the Indians approached the world with a more spiritual bent, putting their faith in the words of their elders and the stories of their people, seeking not to subdue the natural world but to live in harmony with it. Throughout his life he has found himself inspired and guided by this Indian point of view. Many times as an adult, for instance, he has stood with other Native Americans looking across the great expanse of land in South Dakota. Its natural beauty and undefiled landscape is only a memory for him today, for white folk's "progress" has turned the land into a dusty checkerboard of roads and buildings, a land less hospitable to humans and animals than when it was in its natural state.[4]

His parents, Vine and Barbara Deloria, suggested to him that he might study for the Christian ministry like his father and grandfather before him. So, in order to test this possibility, Deloria studied theology at Augustana Lutheran Seminary in Illinois, graduating in 1963 with a Bachelor of Divinity degree. Although well-versed in the teachings of Christianity, he was disappointed that this religion did not speak to the fragmentation and dislocation of the Indian peoples. On the contrary, the history of Christian missions demonstrated to him that Christianity had in large part contributed to the suffering of the Native Americans by seeking to break up the tribes and by taking choice Indian land on which to build churches and schools.

Deloria remembers an encounter he had with a woman at a missionary conference. She sought his advice concerning a particular problem she was facing as a Christian missionary to the Native Americans. In her denomination, the process of conversion required the memorization of the seven steps to salvation. Those who learned it were instructed to teach it to others until Jesus returns in glory. It seems that the young Choctaw pupils in her charge were having difficulty memorizing and reciting the seven steps. She asked Deloria if he had any suggestions for making this task easier.

Well known for his biting wit, Deloria said he could offer her no ideas for getting her students to memorize the seven steps to salvation, but he did suggest that, if she was having so much trouble, she might consider moving on to another mission field that had been better prepared by the Lord. Undeterred, the woman explained that another Christian group had visited the children before her and had left them terribly confused. Not only did she have to spend a great deal of time undoing the work of this other group, but she was determined not to leave the children to another group that might confuse them even more. This, Deloria says, is an example of Christianity's greatest sin against the Native Americans: its insistence on keeping Indian congregations in a perpetual, dependent mission status.[5] These early experiences led Deloria to call for the political and religious self-determination of the native peoples, a theme he expresses repeatedly throughout his writings and teachings.

Following seminary, he took a job with the United Scholarship Service in Denver, where he developed a program that sought to place qualified Indian students in Eastern preparatory schools. His work was often filled with frustration, however, as he encountered opposition from at least two quarters. On the one side were those educators who questioned the "qualifications" of Native American students who often came from the substandard schools provided for them on Indian reservations. On the other side were teachers on the reservations themselves who resisted giving up their best students to schools in the East. Despite the difficulties, Deloria was able to provide advanced educational opportunities to many young people through the program.

From there he served as the executive director of the National Congress of American Indians (NCAI) from 1964 to 1967. Located in Washington, D.C., the NCAI acted as the national voice for all Native Americans. Consequently, the organization was flooded with requests for assistance, though it never had enough funding to meet even a majority of the needs. With the organization constantly on the verge of bankruptcy, Deloria spent much of his time trying to keep the NCAI afloat. At the same time, nearly every effort they made was stonewalled by government officials, many of whom intentionally lied to the Indian peoples.

Even when Deloria was not dealing with those who acted with malice toward the Indians, he did have to contend with well-meaning but unenlightened individuals whose prejudice toward the Native Americans was only thinly concealed. The first year he worked for the NCAI, for example, he and two other Indians paid a visit to a woman, the wife of a member of Congress, who had expressed her desire to become better acquainted with the Indians and their concerns. Deloria was joined on this particular visit by Helen Schierback, a Lumbee, and Imelda Schreiner, a Cheyenne River Sioux. Throughout their afternoon together, the woman asked her guests to repeat their names for her, demonstrating obvious difficulty in remembering them. As she walked them to the door, she asked them again what their names were. With an apology she bid them goodbye, saying, "Indian names are so peculiar and hard to remember."

Deloria reflects that this woman somehow did not even notice that her three guests had European names, probably no different from the names of her closest friends. Her prejudice had blinded her to this fact, however, and had convinced her that these Indians were so exotic and strange that their names had to be impossible to remember.[6]

His experiences with the NCAI demonstrated to him that more than activism and negotiations were needed to safeguard the rights of the Indians to live on their own tribal lands. This belief led him to earn a law degree from the University of Colorado in 1970. He hoped that through legal action and writing about the history and politics of the relationship between Indians and whites he could assist Indians in achieving self-government through education rather than violence.

Deloria embarked on a writing and teaching career that ultimately gave shape and direction to the American Indian movement. He dramatically presented his case for Indian self-determination in his first book, *Custer Died for Your Sins*, written while he was still in law school. In each of his books he carefully documents the historical, political, and spiritual dimensions of the interaction between white leaders and the Native American peoples. Until whites face up to the suffering intentionally inflicted upon Indians and seek to make amends for this mistreatment, Deloria says, the relationship between white folk and red folk will be forever conflicted. His religious views, particularly his frustration with attempts by Christian leaders to destroy Indian culture, are also well represented in most of his books. Throughout his work he highlights the two different worldviews represented by people of European ancestry, shaped by the Judeo-Christian heritage, on the one side, and of the Native Americans on the other, with their emphasis on relationship to the land and the spiritual reality that manifests itself in the natural world. Until whites understand the difference in these two perspectives, Deloria says, whites will never understand Indian culture and religious values.

Deloria's teaching career began at Western Washington State College where he taught from 1970 to 1972. While there he assisted Northwest Coast tribes in their effort to regain fishing rights. From there he went to the University of California at Los Angeles where he taught for the next two years. Concurrently he chaired the Institute for the Development of Indian Law in Washington, D.C., holding that position until 1978 when he became professor of American Indian studies and political science at the University of Arizona. He remained there until 1990 when he joined the faculty of the Center for Studies of Ethnicity and Race in America at the University of Colorado in Boulder.

Although he has been involved with Indian activism for over thirty years, Deloria has no illusions about the vast amount of work still needing to be done in order to restore land and livelihood to displaced Native Americans and to educate people of all races about the truth and the lies surrounding the history of the tribal peoples. One example of such a falsehood is the "overkill" hypothesis espoused by some scientists in North America. The gist of this hypothesis is that the Paleo-Indians, who lived in North America during the end of the last Ice Age, aggressively hunted big game animals, such as mammoths and mastodons. This overkill, the theory suggests, led to the abrupt extinction of these animals in North America approximately ten thousand years ago. Although this hypothesis is built on several shaky foundations, there are those who cling to it tenaciously and actively teach it in universities.

Another example of the challenges Deloria still faces occurred in 1990 when he was invited to speak at Stanford University in California in honor of the school's 100th anniversary. Since he had been asked to speak on the Indian relationship to the land, he put together a talk in which he outlined the philosophical and spiritual values that undergird the Indian view of the natural world. When he completed his talk, he opened the floor to questions. In an obvious reference to the overkill hypothesis, the first questioner asked Deloria whether he thought running a whole herd of buffalo over a hill was wasteful. The tone of the question suggested to him that the questioner thought that Deloria and his Indian friends had spent the last weekend killing bison somewhere in Wyoming! Reflecting on that tense moment at Stanford, Deloria writes that the only slaughter of buffalo he could remember in recent memory took place on Super Bowl Sunday. Greatly offended by the inference of the questioner, he took his seat in protest and refused to answer any further questions.[7]

Despite such disappointing encounters, Deloria's work continues. As an eloquent interpreter of history, politics, and religion in North America, Vine Deloria, Jr., is a man of vision and action, whose heart is rooted in and whose hope is nurtured by the spiritual truth of his people.

READ THE WORDS

As you read the works that follow, ask yourself these questions: What are some ways in which Deloria's writings connect to his life story? How do these words nurture my spiritual life and/or inspire me to engage in acts of social justice?

READING ONE:

Custer Died for Your Sins *was Deloria's first book, written while he was a law student in the late 1960s. Using historical and legal documentation, he carefully lays out the situation of the native peoples of North America, chronicling the trail of broken promises and mistreatment perpetrated by whites. He also expresses the goal of the Indian activist: to become self-ruled, culturally separate from white society and politically separate from the U.S. government. This excerpt is a stinging indictment of "Christian" morality.*

In looking back at the centuries of broken treaties, it is clear that the United States never intended to keep any of its promises. Like other areas of life, the federal government adapted its policies to the expediency of the moment. When the crisis had passed, it promptly proceeded on its way without a backward glance at its treachery.

Indian people have become extremely wary of promises made by the federal government. The past has shown them that even the most innocent-looking proposal is often fraught with implications the sum total of which is loss of land.

Too often the attitude of the white man was, "Tell the Indians anything to keep them quiet. After they are settled down we can do what we want to do."

"What," people often ask, "did you expect to happen? After all, the continent had to be settled, didn't it?"

We always reply, "Did it?" And continue, "If it did, did it have to be settled in that way?" For if you consider it, the continent is now settled and yet uninhabitable in many places today...

The betrayal of treaty promises has in this generation created a greater feeling of unity among Indian people than any other subject. There is not a single tribe that does not burn with resentment over the treatment it has received at the hands of an avowedly *Christian* nation. New incidents involving treaty rights daily remind Indian people that they were betrayed by a government which insists on keeping up the façade of maintaining its commitments in Vietnam.

The complicity of the churches too is just beginning to be recognized. After several hundred years of behind-the-scenes machinations, the attempt of the churches to appear relevant to the social needs of the 1960s is regarded as utter hypocrisy by many Indian people. If, they argue, the churches actually wanted justice, why haven't they said or done anything about Indian rights?

Until America begins to build a moral record in her dealings with the Indian people she should not try to fool the rest of the world about her intentions on other continents. America has always been a militantly imperialistic world power eagerly grasping for economic control over weaker nations.

The Indian wars of the past should rightly be regarded as the first foreign wars of American history. As the United States marched across this continent, it was creating an empire by wars of foreign conquest just as England and France were doing in India and Africa. Certainly the war with Mexico was imperialistic, no more or less than the wars against the Sioux, Apache, Utes, and Yakimas. In every case the goal was identical: land...

When one considers American history in its imperialistic light, it becomes apparent that if morality is to be achieved in this country's relations with other nations a return to basic principles is in order. Definite commitments to fulfill extant treaty obligations to Indian tribes would be the first step toward introducing morality into American foreign policy.[8]

READING TWO:

In We Talk, You Listen *Deloria addresses the difficulties of communication between red and white folk and calls for a return to tribalism in order for Indian society to thrive, let alone survive. In this next excerpt, written at the height of the black civil rights movement, Deloria describes the differences between the situation of black people and Indians in America.*

The whole of American society has been brainwashed into believing that if it understood blacks it could automatically understand every other group simply because blacks were the most prominent minority group with which white society had to deal. Many whites are therefore stunned when they discover the current Indian slogan of "leave us alone." In the white-black terminology this is a threatening phrase because it implies that no contact should occur between races. Blacks have not had to suffer the stifling paternalism that Indians have suffered from churches, universities, and state and federal governments. Blacks have been able to develop their own version of religion, including liturgy and congregational participation, that answers their needs. Indians have been systematically denied this right.

While blacks have had to fight for legal rights to develop their own institutions, Indians have had a multitude of institutions that were ostensibly theirs, yet they have been deprived of the right to operate them in the way that the in people saw fit. Blacks have had the advantage of alliances with elements of white society on a nearly equal basis. During the civil rights struggle young whites came South and worked with black people because they believed in the fight for equal rights and because they felt that integration was God's will. But whites coming to Indian country came primarily to "experience" Indians. I spoke at a conference of educators one year and described the reservations and how we needed specific help in educational projects. After the talk a woman came gushing up to me and said that she was so interested in having a work camp go out to Indian country because she wanted her children to have THAT EXPERIENCE.

Now I could think of a lot of exotic experiences that Indians could provide for wandering college students with a summer to kill. But it is damn depressing to realize that your tribe exists at the sufferance of a society because it can be experienced.[9]

READING THREE:

God Is Red, *published in 1973, contains Deloria's interpretation of the ways in which Christianity has failed the Native American peoples. From his extensive study of theology and religious experience, he believes that Indians need to return primarily to traditional spiritual values. At the same time, Christians need to become more open to the truth that is found in other religions.*

Many thoughtful and useful systems of belief of ancient peoples have been simply rejected *a priori* by Western thinkers in the religious sphere. This attitude has intruded into Western science and then emerged as criteria by which the world of our experience is judged, condemned, and too often sentenced to death. Many people, for example, have developed astrological systems by which they have charted the nature of relationships between the lives of men and the movement of the planets and stars. Given that modern science now views the universe as an extremely sophisticated electromagnetic complex, the contentions of astrologers as to the influence of the heavens on individual propensities to behave in certain ways may not be as superstitious as it would at first appear. Yet astrology is rejected out of hand by many followers of Western religious thinking because it conflicts with the philosophical problem of free will.

For centuries the Chinese have used and practiced acupuncture as a regular part of their religious and cultural beliefs. The very idea that there might be centers of feeling within the human body that can block off pain and sensation if properly understood was virtually anathema to many Westerners...

All of these things have been excluded from our consideration. We have been taught to consider problems using logic and concepts that ignore certain facets of existence. Religious experiences are not nearly as important to Western man as his creeds, theologies, and speculations—all products of the intellect and not necessarily based on experiences...

What are religious experiences? Are they of such a nature that they can only be described in terms of the Western peoples, or do they properly belong in non-Western categories? It is a fact that many societies of man have had definable and satisfactory relationships with some form of divinity almost from the beginning of mankind's journey on the planet. Traditional Western thought, and more specifically traditional Christian thought, has been based on the assumption that these religions have often been cruel delusions perpetrated against primitive societies by religious leaders, *shamans*, and medicine men seeking personal gain or additional powers, or men forced into trickery to preserve their place in society.

We cannot conclude that other peoples spent centuries in a state of delusion simply because their experiences of God were so different than those of Western peoples. That their experiences could not be either described accurately by Westerners or understood in Western categories of thought does not make them false. The least we can do is to understand that it is in the nature of religion to exert a profound influence within societies and groups and sustain the community or national group over a period of time. Having retreated even that much, the Western world must be prepared to analyze religion as a phenomenon that does not necessarily explain the unanswered questions posed by the philosophical mind, but which may, in itself, cause such questions to occur to all manner of men in a great variety of situations.[10]

READING FOUR:

In The Metaphysics of Modern Existence, *Deloria questions the Western ways of viewing modern life and outlines a worldview based on Native American values. In the introduction he offers a general comparison of Indian and non-Indian perspectives of reality.*

The fundamental facet that keeps Indians and non-Indians from communicating is that they are speaking about two entirely different perceptions of the world. Growing up on an Indian reservation makes one acutely aware of the mysteries of the universe. Medicine men practicing their ancient ceremonies perform feats that amaze and puzzle the rational mind. The sense of contentment enjoyed by older Indians in the face of a lifetime's experience of betrayal, humiliation, and paternalism stuns the astute observer. It often appears that Indians are immune to the values which foreign institutions have forced them to confront. Their minds remain fixed on other realities...

No matter how well educated an Indian may become, he or she always suspects that Western culture is not an adequate representation of reality. Life therefore becomes a schizophrenic balancing act wherein one holds that the creation, migration, and ceremonial stories of the tribe are true and that the Western European view of the world is also true. Obviously this situation is impossible although just how it becomes impossible remains a mystery to most Indians. The trick is somehow to relate what one *feels* to what one is taught to *think.* Western peoples seem to have little difficulty doing this since accumulating knowledge is for them an initiatory act that admits them to higher status employment. They do not seem concerned with the ultimate truth of what they are taught. Indians, for the most part, fail to comprehend the sanity of this attitude at all...

The natural response of Indians, including myself, has been to accept those dissident and heretical theories of Western culture that seem to correlate and support the Indian interpretation of the meaning of life. In recent years this has not been a difficult task. Modern physicists, incapable of expressing space-time perception in the English language, now often refer to the Zuni or Hopi conception of space-time as the more accurate rendering of what they are finding at the subatomic level of experiments. Psychoanalysts, working with dream theories, are now more inclined to view the dream-interpretation systems of the Cherokee and the Iroquois as consistent and highly significant methods of handling certain types of mental and emotional problems. Geologists, attempting to understand the history of rivers and volcanoes, are now turning to Indian legends in an effort to gain some perspective on the problems...

If an Indian tells other Indians that he or she has seen a ghost, describes the experience, and asks others for advice, he or she is taken to be a serious person with a serious problem. However if a non-Indian tells another non-Indian that he or she has seen a ghost, it is another matter entirely. Scientists will give the person a suspicious look and recommend a psychiatrist. The priest or minister will take great pains to reassure the person that he or she in fact did *not* see a ghost...

Therein lies the difference: The Indian confronts the reality of the experience, and while he or she may not make immediate sense of it, it is not rejected as an invalid experience. In the Indian world, experience is not limited by mental consideration and assumptions regarding the universe. For the non-Indian the teachings of a lifetime come thundering down. Such things do not occur in time and space. Reality is basically physical. No one sees ghosts. Reality, in a certain sense, is what you allow your mind to accept, not what you experience.[11]

REFLECT AND ACT

By yourself, or in cooperation with others, engage in the following reflection and action exercises. Try to do one exercise each day for a week. If one activity is particularly meaningful, stay with it for a longer period of time. Also feel free to create exercises of your own as you are inspired by the life and witness of Vine Deloria, Jr.

1. Read again the Lakota creation story as told at the beginning of this chapter. Compare it to the creation story of your religious tradition. Going to a place in nature—a forest, a garden, a park, a hiking trail, or your backyard—meditate on

the sacred aspect of the natural world. Watch, listen, and feel for God's presence in the surroundings you have chosen.

2. Much of Deloria's work is based on what he perceives to be a marked difference between the Western and Indian worldviews. Look at his life story and especially Reading Four for a description of these two perspectives. List the main features of each of these on a piece of paper or a chalkboard. How are these worldviews supported or ridiculed by various aspects of society—the government, business, educational systems—and religious groups? Which perspective feels most comfortable to you? Why? Are they mutually exclusive, or are there ways in which they can be reconciled or complementary?

3. Reflect on the hostile context of Deloria's childhood, in which signs stating "No Dogs and No Indians" were prominently displayed. Imagine yourself as a child reading a sign that says "No Dogs and No _____," inserting your own racial or religious group. Write about your reflections using the following questions: How would you feel about yourself and the world into which you were born? How would the adults around you react to discrimination? How would your future be affected by the limitations placed upon you?

4. Deloria often uses humor to call attention to injustices and to lessen tension. Watch a comedy routine by a comedian known for his or her biting social commentary, such as George Carlin or Dennis Miller. How does their humor bring out into the open those issues that are hidden and rarely spoken about? Does their sarcasm grab your attention or make you want to turn away?

5. Think back throughout your life and remember those places that were spiritually significant for you, such as a childhood home, a house of worship, a certain park, or a site where a particular event occurred. What characteristics set that place apart from other places? How do you feel about yourself and your world when you are in that place? What form does divine presence take in that sacred place?

6. Read a classic book in Indian history, such as Dee Brown's *Bury My Heart at Wounded Knee,* or Indian spirituality, such

as *Black Elk Speaks* by John Neihardt. What is the role of the spoken word (oral tradition) in Native American culture in contrast to the emphasis on the written word in Western society? How does the wisdom and knowledge of tribal elders contribute to the Indians' understanding of history and the building of community?

7. In Reading Three above, Deloria describes religion as "a phenomenon that does not necessarily explain the unanswered questions...but which...cause[s] such questions to occur." Meditate on the unanswered questions of your life. Choose one such question and reflect on the ways in which your religious tradition helps you to resolve this question in some satisfactory way. What resources are available to you to make it possible to live with the unanswered questions of life? Close your meditation time by thanking God for the mysteries of the world.

8. Return to the 1960s through newspaper or magazine accounts, or by watching a television documentary. During this time period the United States witnessed the rise of both the black civil rights movement and the American Indian self-determination movement. Explore the role of organized religion as it encouraged or thwarted the work of these two groups. You can even gather some firsthand information by interviewing someone who was involved in one or both of these movements. In what ways were religious groups willing to speak out and act against injustice? In what ways were they hesitant? Why did they respond differently to the American Indians than to the black Americans?

9. Immerse yourself in Indian art forms, either by visiting a local museum that is exhibiting Native American art, looking through an art book, or attending a performance of ceremonial dance. Look at this art from a spiritual and emotional, not an intellectual and analytical, point of view. How does it speak to you and put you in touch with divine presence? Using pen and ink, watercolors, clay, or another medium, create your own art, feeling free to use Indian motifs or any symbols that express your own spiritual reality. Try to maintain a lighthearted and playful attitude throughout this

exercise, allowing yourself to be open to the guidance of the Great Spirit.

10. Research the history of the native peoples who once lived (or may continue to live) in the vicinity of your home. How large was their tribe? What can you learn about their way of life and religious beliefs? When were they displaced from the land? How did this dislocation occur? Where are descendants of the tribe living today? What are the customs and concerns of their everyday life today? If you are so moved, consider making contact with members of the tribe as a gesture of friendship and care.

11. Invite a Native American storyteller to meet with your group to share the inspiring Indian legends that have been passed down in oral form through the generations. As an alternative, meet together for a storytelling celebration in which each person shares a legend, story, prayer, or song from one of the many books and albums that have been published. Especially look for Indian stories among children's books, most of which are beautifully illustrated as well.

FOR FURTHER READING

Carmody, Denise Lardner and John Tully Carmody. *Native American Religions: An Introduction.* New York: Paulist Press, 1993.

Deloria, Vine, Jr. *Custer Died for Your Sins: An Indian Manifesto.* New York: Macmillan Company, 1969.

———. *We Talk, You Listen: New Tribes, New Turf.* New York: Macmillan Company, 1970.

———. *God Is Red.* New York: Grosset and Dunlap, 1973.

———. *Behind the Trail of Broken Treaties.* New York: Delacorte Press, 1974.

———. *The Metaphysics of Modern Existence.* San Francisco: Harper and Row, 1979.

———. *Red Earth, White Lies: Native Americans and the Myth of Scientific Fact.* New York: Scribner Books, 1995.

Notes

[1]The Lakota are one of three groups of North American Plains Indians collectively known as Sioux. The other two groups are called Nakota and Dakota. See Denise Lardner Carmody and John Tully Carmody, *Native American Religions* (New York: Paulist Press, 1993), 258 and 261–62.

[2]Jack LaPointe, *Legends of the Lakota* (San Francisco: Indian Historian Press, 1976), 14–15.

[3]Vine Deloria, Jr., *God Is Red* (New York: Grosset and Dunlap, 1973), 25.

[4]Vine Deloria, Jr., *Custer Died for Your Sins* (New York: The Macmillan Company, 1969), 103–4.

[5]Ibid., 111–12.

[6]Vine Deloria, Jr., *We Talk, You Listen* (New York: The Macmillan Company, 1970), 25–26.

[7]Vine Deloria, Jr., *Red Earth, White Lies* (New York: Scribner, 1995), 110–13.

[8]Deloria, *Custer Died for Your Sins*, 48–49, 50, 51.

[9]Deloria, *We Talk, You Listen*, 88–89.

[10]Deloria, *God Is Red*, 290–91, 292–93.

[11]Vine Deloria, Jr., *The Metaphysics of Modern Existence* (San Francisco: Harper and Row, 1979), vii–xi.

Chapter Eight

Joanna Macy

At One with the Natural World

PREPARE TO MEDITATE

This contemplation on nature may take one of three forms: Go to a park, some woods, or an ocean where you can experience the beauty and power of the natural world; look at a picture of nature or one of the many beings that inhabit the planet; or quietly image a place or being in your mind, paying attention to all the details, including color, scent, and sound. Choose one aspect of your experience—a tree, an animal, an insect, the wind—and imagine that you are that thing. In your meditative encounter with the natural world, move beyond merely seeing it and seek to become one with it.

HEAR THE STORIES

Joanna Macy was born Joanna Rogers in Los Angeles in 1929, but she grew up in New York City. A nature lover from her earliest days, she remembers her childhood as an unhappy one, mainly because there was too much concrete in the city. Her salvation was her summer vacations at her grandfather's farm in western New York State. There she joyfully spent time with her best friends: two trees and a horse. During the rest of the year she attended French primary and secondary school in Manhattan, often being the only native-born American in her classes.

113

Macy came from a long line of Presbyterian ministers, the last one being her grandfather. She was deeply touched by her grandfather's devotion to the church. At the age of sixteen she underwent a pivotal mystical encounter in which she experienced being present with Christ at his crucifixion. This experience occurred against the backdrop of a world feeling the shock of two world wars and the Holocaust, as well as an urban community dealing with the stress of poverty and crime. In that moment she realized the depth of human suffering—not only the pain many people feel but the incredible ability of people to inflict pain on others. What happened to Jesus, she discovered, can happen to anyone. Even more, we can recognize our own participation in the crucifixion. She says of that realization, "My life wasn't 'mine' in the same way ever again."[1]

As an undergraduate at Wellesley College, Macy studied biblical history hoping to become a missionary to Africa. One day she was privileged to meet Albert Schweitzer, the world-renowned physician and philosopher who had founded a hospital in the African jungle. She acted as his interpreter during his trip to New York City, and she continued to correspond with him while she was in college. Later in life he became a leader in the call for nuclear disarmament, a subject that eventually came to guide Macy's path toward activism as well. Although Schweitzer's strong witness taught Macy the deep reverence for life within the Christian faith, Macy soon became disillusioned with Christianity's exclusivism toward people of other beliefs. Not knowing where else to turn for spiritual guidance, she became an atheist.

During her senior year in college Macy went to France on a Fulbright Scholarship. There she studied political science, particularly Marxism and French Communist Party tactics. Upon her return to the United States she secured a job with the State Department as an intelligence analyst. Appalled at discrimination in 1950s America, she became involved in the civil rights movement and the struggle to end discrimination in housing.

While working in Washington, Macy met her husband-to-be, Fran Macy, a Soviet affairs analyst. They lived in Munich for five years when Fran's work took him there. Then, when he joined the staff of the Peace Corps, Fran and Joanna moved with their three children to India. By now it was the mid-1960s and the United States was just getting involved in the war in Vietnam. While in India, Macy grew to know Tibetan refugees, victims of brutal Chinese repression, living hand-to-mouth in crowded bungalows in Dalhousie. There she worked with American Peace Corps volunteers to help the Tibetans produce handmade crafts that they hoped to sell worldwide.

One day, she accompanied her oldest son to a class on Buddhist teachings. During that particular lesson, the English-speaking nun teaching the class instructed the students in an exercise in compassion. Reminding them that all sentient beings go through a cycle of birth and rebirth, she reflected that at some point in that ongoing process each being was our mother. To cultivate compassion toward others, she then invited them to practice viewing each person as their mother in a former life. Macy walked back home, reflecting on this interesting exercise. Too bad I don't believe in reincarnation, she mused, otherwise this might be a fun experiment.

As this thought crossed her mind, she met up with a coolie journeying along the same path as she. Under normal circumstances, the sight of a coolie made her turn away in anger and disgust. Coolies are load-bearing laborers, usually seen carrying heavy logs up steep mountain paths. Macy decried a social system that relegated certain people to such menial, back-breaking tasks. But that afternoon, fresh from the class on compassion, she looked upon him differently. She looked upon him as her mother, the one who had given birth to her in another lifetime. She strained to see the features of his face, bent down under a heavy load. She looked lovingly at his gnarled hands, dirty clothes, and head wrapped in a turban. Her mind suddenly filled with questions about where he was going, who was waiting for him when he arrived there, and whether or not his home was filled with love and happiness. She says that even as they passed one another on that mountain path, she did nothing to change his life. But things had changed markedly for her as compassion filled her heart.[2]

This, and other experiences like it, prompted Macy to attend a retreat atop a Himalayan mountain. Drawn to the Buddhist teaching of the interdependence of all beings and the practice of meditation to awaken that awareness, she found her interest in religion and spirituality reawakened. The following encounter with a Buddhist teacher demonstrates the insight and depth of compassion that Macy saw in the spiritual teaching and practice of Buddhism.

One summer afternoon in Dalhousie she and others had a meeting with the Tibetan monks to discuss plans for securing grants and founding a self-sufficient settlement of refugees. As usual, Macy approached the meeting with urgency, wanting to make plans and accomplish the goals that had been set. In stark contrast to Macy's inner anxiety, however, the monks peacefully drank their tea, one monk even painting on a canvas he had placed beside himself. At some point in the gathering, she looked into her teacup to discover that a fly had fallen into her drink. She must have winced at the discovery for one of the monks, eighteen-year-old Choegyal Rinpoche, asked her what was wrong. Thinking of herself as a seasoned traveler in India and not wanting to give the impression that she was afraid of a little insect, she smiled at Choegyal and said laughingly, "Oh, nothing. It's just a fly in my tea."

Although the meeting continued on around them, Choegyal took great interest in the fly in Macy's tea. He got up from his seat and gently placed one finger into her teacup to remove the bug and then left the room. Macy gave little thought to the monk's actions. After all, she was concerned with the important decisions that had to be made that day. How surprised she was when Choegyal returned to the meeting, a broad smile gracing his face. He whispered to Macy, "He is going to be all right." He then explained how he had placed the fly on a leaf to allow him to dry his wings in the sun. When Choegyal saw that the little insect was able to fan his wings gently to speed the drying process, he knew that the fly would recover from his fall into the tea.

Macy says that she remembers little of the work that was accomplished in the meeting that day, but she does remember Choegyal's act of compassion on behalf of a being that most of us would view as insignificant and annoying. How wonderful, she thought, if I could know the joy of expressing concern for all beings, even flies.[3]

Concerns such as this prompted Macy to return to graduate school, earning a Ph.D. from Syracuse University in 1978. In her studies she sought to bring together two theories, one of Western origin and another from the East. The Western theory was that of general systems, a theory that looks at various types of systems—biological, social, cognitive, and ecological—and studies how they organize themselves and interrelate with one another. Systems are not just described as the sum of their parts but instead are seen in their wholeness. The Eastern theory is actually a Buddhist teaching known by its Pali name *paticca samuppada,* meaning "dependent coorigination." Quite simply, this doctrine teaches that all beings are interdependent with one another. From her studies she discovered a whole new way of looking at the world, one that compelled her to become more deeply involved in social causes. If it is true that all things are interdependent and that a change in one part of a system causes changes in other parts of the system as well, then what we do, no matter how big or small, *does* make a difference!

In addition to protesting U.S. military involvement in Vietnam, Macy soon became involved in environmental causes, particularly the use of nuclear power and the stockpiling of nuclear weapons. She participated in protests at nuclear reactors throughout the United States, attempting to call attention to the threat of nuclear annihilation and the dangers of nuclear waste. As a result of the protests, however, she found herself descending into a state of despair in which she experienced a profound sense of grief for herself, all of humankind, and the whole planet. One of her first experiences with "despair-work" occurred just about the time that U.S. forces were preparing to leave Vietnam. One spring afternoon she was feeling particularly depleted. Tired of speaking, reading, and writing, she took out a hunk of clay, hoping to give expression to her feelings without using words. Filled with sadness and anger, her fingers formed mountains and valleys, her fists pounded the clay into nothingness. When she felt she had done all she could, her thoughts turned to other things, but her hands continued to work the clay. As she watched with wonder, her fingers gave shape to roots. Although roots exist underground and are hidden from view, she pondered, they are strong and firm, the very foundation of life. Despite her despair, the roots spoke to her of the possibility of hope.[4]

This experience motivated Macy to do additional despair-work. Recognizing that pain can be a healthy sign of warning as well as of potential growth, she adapted Buddhist meditation techniques to awaken and work through this emotional pain. When she wrote an article about her personal despair-work for a magazine in 1979, she was bombarded with letters from people interested in doing despair-work of their own. As a result, she developed "Despair and Empowerment" workshops, which she has subsequently conducted all over the world.

After leading one such workshop in England, she visited Greenham Common and other U.S. missile bases in Europe. There she saw a familiar sight, people camped out in tents to protest the use of nuclear power and especially the existence of nuclear weapons. She was familiar with this because of her own participation in anti-nuclear protests, calling attention not only to the horrible threat of nuclear annihilation but to the danger of nuclear poisoning from toxins that leak into the air, soil, and water supply. On this occasion, however, she saw the protest in a different light. She saw the nuclear sites not as places of desolation, but as spiritual places. She recognized that the people were not protesters as much as they were pilgrims, many of whom had traveled long distances to come to this place.

From this realization arose the idea for Guardian Sites, places to which concerned people would journey to express their hope for the future of our world. Rather than turn away in horror and fear, these people would come to nuclear silos and nuclear power plants as if they were making a pilgrimage to a holy monastery. There the people would join together to test the soil and water to make certain that radioactive levels were in a safe range for humans and animals. There they would witness to the choice that humankind is called to make, a choice for life or for death.[5]

Standing outside a nuclear site holding a sign of protest does not seem to many to be a very significant act. However, Macy sees this one simple act as a way in which one person can bear witness to the dangers threatening the entire planet. What looks like a small action to others is actually a large one for that individual who carries it out. She reminds us that everything we do, whether small or large, affects the entire world and all who dwell in it. This means that we do not have to go to the source in order to solve the world's problems. Instead, because everything exists in a web of interdependent relationships, we can jump in anywhere, wherever we may find ourselves, and bring about change for the better.

This yearning for a hopeful future was expressed by Macy and others at the close of a workshop on ecology held during the mid-1980s in England. Environmental activists from a myriad of social and religious backgrounds had come together to discuss the future of our beleaguered planet and to encourage one another in their respective efforts to heal the world. Social workers, teachers, homemakers, Jews, Christians, Buddhists, and pagans stood together on a drizzly morning, forming a human circle around ancient, standing stones, long revered for their sacred power. She says that in that moment it was as if they realized a dual perspective on time. On the one hand, being in the presence of sacred stones thousands of years old prodded them to seek the wisdom of old Mother Earth. On the other hand, their presence in the here and now compelled them to face the ways in which the planet is being destroyed in countless big and little ways each and every day. In that moment, they experienced a bonding with the Earth and with one another. Despite the differences in their religious beliefs, they expressed a shared commitment to a physical and spiritual renewal of the Earth and all beings.[6]

This, then, is the hope that Joanna Macy expresses through her writings, workshops, and activism. Through Guardian Sites, Despair and Empowerment Workshops, and Deep Ecology she calls us to sense the deep interconnections among all that exists, and to join her in her healing work for their sake and for ours.

READ THE WORDS

As you read the works that follow, ask yourself these questions: What are some ways in which Macy's writings connect to her life story? How do these words nurture my spiritual life and/or inspire me to engage in acts of social justice?

READING ONE:

Macy's studies and interests carried her back and forth between two poles, the spiritual and the political. All the religions and social systems that she encountered always stressed one or the other, but never both, of these two dimensions. She was delighted to discover the Sarvodaya movement in Sri Lanka. In this Buddhist-inspired self-help movement, founded by A. T. Ariyaratna, the spiritual and the political converge. For a year in the late 1970s she lived and worked in Sri Lanka studying the religious roots of Sarvodaya. Her book Dharma and Development *chronicles what she discovered there as well as how what has been successful in Sri Lanka might be useful in our part of the world. This first selection is called "To Listen to the People."*

Ariyaratna says, "A country cannot develop unless one has faith in the intelligence of the people." How is this intelligence tapped?

It was with the villagers first and foremost, not the urban elite or the government officials, that Ariyaratna and his colleagues sought to communicate; and since true communication is a two-way street, that meant listening, too. To listen with attention and respect is a skill which the Movement stressed, emphasizing that it is the villagers themselves who are, in the last analysis, the "experts" on what they need and what they can do. Instead of coming in with preformulated blue-prints for action, organizers, as we have seen, instigate "family gatherings" where the local community itself assesses its needs and determines its priorities by consensus. These provide, sometimes for the first time, the occasion where a broad cross-section of villagers can listen to each other, too. Out of this interaction has grown the fresh and deceptively simple formulations through which Sarvodaya conveys its philosophy of development.

A striking feature of the many Sarvodaya organizers I knew was their respect for the common man, woman, or child at the grassroots level. They appeared able to see value in each person's experience and perspective, whatever his background or extent of formal schooling. Their ability to do so—to perceive and accord value—may be reinforced by the Sarvodayan practice of *metta,* the lovingkindness meditation which breeds respect for all beings; but, in any case, it has permitted people in over four thousand villages to feel that they count and that they have some kind of ownership in Sarvodaya's programs.

In my own country many concerned and well-intentioned people do not act on social problems, because they feel they do not have the "answers" to them. Sarvodaya reminds us that pre-fabricated solutions are unnecessary and even dysfunctional, and that what we really need to do is to go to the people, generate communication, and be unafraid to listen.[7]

READING TWO:

This second excerpt from Dharma and Development, *entitled "To Integrate Spiritual and Social Change," describes the way in which the spiritual and the political converge in the Sarvodaya movement.*

Sarvodaya's dynamism derives to a large extent...from its capacity to merge people's spiritual aspirations with engagement in community action. Seeking to "awaken" both person and society, its values aim for individual fulfillment as well as social transformation. Although I had expected otherwise, imagining that they resided mainly in headquarters rhetoric, I found these values to be vital and self-generating among grassroots workers. Their comments and behavior conveyed a simple, bold, matter-of-fact assumption that through engagement in Sarvodaya's programs, their fellow-beings can transform their experience of who they are and how they relate to each other. For most this belief is basic to a continuing personal commitment that has few, if any, material awards.

Such a wholistic view of social change is pertinent to industrialized societies as well where the old conceptual dichotomies that divided the personal and spiritual from the social and political are beginning to erode. In cultures plagued by alienation and despair there is a hunger for the sense of meaning, belonging, and hope that such an integration can bring. Indeed, there are many signs that it is occurring, in a convergence of concerns. The 1960s in America generated a surge of social reform efforts (in the civil rights and antiwar movements); the 1970s saw a shift to the search for more personal transformation (in the human potential and spiritual awareness movements).

A convergence of these two currents is evident in the 1980s, as increasing numbers of people on the local level turn to concerns for peace and social justice, but within the context of spiritual growth. Religious beliefs are being rearticulated in social terms, as people seek guidance and support in reshaping their lives and their society.[8]

READING THREE:

Mutual Causality in Buddhism and General Systems Theory is a scholarly book based on Macy's doctoral studies. In it she describes the interdependence of all phenomena, drawing from the Buddhist doctrine of paticca samuppada (dependent co-arising) and the Western theory of general systems. "The tree and the flame" are powerful symbols of mutual causality and interdependence.

Two images appear both in general systems theory and early Buddhist teachings, as these two bodies convey their vision of mutual causality. These are the tree and the flame.

We encountered the tree image in general systems theory. Symbolic of the manner in which systems and subsystems hierarchically structure themselves, growing out of and into each other like trunk and branches and limbs, the tree represents relationship. It images the multiformity and unity of our interconnectedness as holons, from atom to person to community and ecosystem.

Tree is also a dominant feature in early Buddhist imagery. There it appears both as *bodhi* tree, under which Gotama [the given name of the Buddha] sat and gained enlightenment, and as the wishing tree which, laden with the good things of life, bestows the answers to our hearts' desires. Originating as a motif in early Indian tree-worship, it came then to symbolize for the Buddhist world both wisdom and plenty, consciousness *and* nature…

Our second image, flame…appeared at the outset of general systems theory…to convey how the open system endures in shape while constantly altered by metabolic events. As the open system consumes the matter that passes through it, burning it, so metaphorically does it process information—ever breaking down and building up, renewed. Like fire, it both transforms and is transformed by that on which it feeds. Flame then represents the metabolic nature of life, and the nature of our identity as selves.

This metaphor features in the Buddha Dharma [teaching] as well, from the first teaching the Buddha gave at Gaya, the fire sermon. "Everything, O Bikkhus, is burning..." Later when he explained the arising of consciousness the image of flame was also employed, the mind igniting and feeding on sensory perceptions like a fire burning from grass or sticks. And when selfhood is extinguished, it is like a candle blown out...

What have tree and flame to do with the ethics of mutual causality? Significant to both general systems theory and early Buddhist teachings, these images serve to convey the interdependence of our lives and also the process by which transformation takes place. Or, to put it another way, they symbolize the reciprocal interplay of structure and process. Like roots, trunk and branches, we beings are interconnected and part of each other. Our griefs and hopes are not separate, nor can our fulfillments be private, for we are as organically linked as a tree. To act with this knowledge, and shape our lives and institutions to reflect it, requires transformations that threaten our comfort and security. It requires a dying to old ways. This is easier to accept and face when we realize that, like a flame, we are ever dying and renewing, for that is the nature of things.[9]

READING FOUR:

Macy's book World as Lover, World as Self, *is a collection of articles about Buddhist teachings and her own learnings while in Asia and other parts of the world. In this excerpt from an article entitled "Faith, Power and Ecology," she discusses one of the important discoveries necessary for faith to be possible.*

We are experiencers of compassion. Buddhism has a term for that kind of being—it is *bodhisattva*. The bodhisattva is the Buddhist model for heroic behavior. Knowing there is no such thing as private salvation, she or he does not hold aloof from this suffering world or try to escape from it. It is a question rather of returning again and again to work on behalf of all beings, because the bodhisattva knows there is no healing or transformation without connection.

The *sutras*, or scriptures, tell us that we are all bodhisattvas, and our fundamental interconnections are portrayed in the beautiful image of the Jeweled Net of Indra. It is similar to the holographic model of the universe we find emerging from contemporary science. In the cosmic canopy of Indra's Net, each of us, each jewel at each node of the net, reflects all the others and reflects the others reflecting back. That is what we find when we listen to the sounds of the Earth crying within us—that the tears that arise are not ours alone; they are the tears of an Iraqi mother looking for her children in the rubble; they are the tears of a Navajo uranium miner learning that he is dying of lung cancer. We find we are interwoven threads in the intricate tapestry of life, its deep ecology.

What happens for us then is what every major religion has sought to offer—a shift in identification, a shift from the isolated "I" to a new, vaster sense of what we are. This is understandable not only as a spiritual experience, but also, in scientific terms, as an evolutionary development. As living forms evolve on this planet, we move not only in the direction of diversification, but toward integration as well. Indeed, these two movements complement and enhance each other. Open systems self-organize and integrate by virtue of their differentiation, and, vice-versa, they differentiate by virtue of their interactions. As we evolved we progressively shed our shells, our armor, our separate encasements; we grew soft, sensitive, vulnerable protuberances, like eyes, lips, and fingertips, to better connect and receive information, to better know and interweave our knowings. If we are all bodhisattvas, it is because that thrust to connect, that capacity to integrate with and through each other, is our true nature.[10]

READING FIVE:

"In League with the Beings of the Future" is another selection from World as Lover, World as Self. *She looks at the future not just in terms of what legacy we would like to leave for those who come after us, but according to what future beings would like us to leave for them.*

> "For you shall be in league with the stones of the field,
>   and the beasts of the field shall be at peace with you"
>   (Job 5:23).

This verse of the Bible delighted me as a child and stayed with me as I grew up. It promised a way I wanted to live—in complicity with creation. It still comes to mind when I hear about people taking action on behalf of other species. When our brothers and sisters of Greenpeace or Earth First! put their lives on the line to save the whales or the old-growth forests, I think, "Ah, they're in league."

To be "in league" in that way seems wonderful. There is a comfortable, cosmic collegiality to it—like coming home to conspire once more with our beloved and age-old companions, with the stones and the beasts of the field, and the sun that rises and the stars revolving in the sky.

Now the work of restoring ravaged Earth offers us that—and with a new dimension. It not only puts us in league with the stones and the beasts, but also in league with the beings of the future. All that we do for the mending of our planet is for their sake, too. Their chance to live and love our world depends in large measure on us and our often uncertain efforts.

I sense those beings of the future times hovering, like a cloud of witnesses. Sometimes I fancy that if I were to turn my head suddenly, I would glimpse them over my shoulder—they and their claim on life have become that real to me. Philosophers and mystics say that chronological time is a construct, a function of our mentality; there is also, they say, a dimension in which all time is simultaneous, where we co-exist with past and future. Perhaps because I am so time-ridden, hurrying to meet this deadline and that appointment, I am drawn to that notion. The dimension of simultaneity, where we stand shoulder to shoulder with our ancestors and descendants, is appealing to me, it gives context and momentum to work for social change.

In that context it is plausible to me that the generations of the future want to lend us courage for what we do for their sake. I imagine them saying "thanks" for our dogged efforts to protect the rainforests. Thanks for our citizen campaigns on behalf of the seas and rivers. Thanks for working on renewable energy sources, so that those who come after us can have breathable air.

The imagined presence of these future ones comes to me like grace and works upon my life. That is one reason why I have been increasingly drawn to the issue of radioactive waste.

Of the many causes that pull us into league with the future, this one, in terms of time and toxicity, is the most enduring legacy our generation will leave behind.[11]

REFLECT AND ACT

By yourself, or in cooperation with others, engage in the following reflection and action exercises. Try to do one exercise each day for a week. If one activity is particularly meaningful, stay with it for a longer period of time. Also feel free to create your own exercises as you are inspired by the life and witness of Joanna Macy.

1. Look again at Macy's description of the tree and flame as images that symbolize mutual causality in general systems theory and Buddhist teaching (Reading Three). What other images for interdependence can you develop? Choose one image and express it creatively by drawing a picture, composing a song, or acting out a pantomime.

2. Imagine a conversation with a being who lives in the future—your own unborn child or grandchild, a person your age living two hundred years from now, an animal, or a familiar land formation. What is the world of the future like? What are this being's joys, sorrows, frustrations, and hopes? What is this being asking of you as the current caretaker of the world?

3. Note the way in which Macy's involvement in social causes shifted to coincide with changes in society, from civil rights to anti-war activism to environmental awareness. Looking at the social scene today, what causes seem to be most crucial? What religious, cultural, social, and personal factors contribute to your choice?

4. Participate in *metta*, a loving-kindness meditation. Sit quietly, concentrating on the gentle rhythm of your breathing. Begin by expressing loving-kindness toward yourself, even those parts you think are unlovable—body parts, emotions, or actions. Do not judge yourself, but be filled with compassion for who and what you are. Then, practice *metta* when expressing concern for someone else. Finally, practice *metta* when experiencing conflict with another person. This third

form of meditation has a way of easing tensions, both within your own mind and between you and the other person.

5. Certain well-known people had tremendous influence on Macy, particularly Albert Schweitzer and A. T. Ariyaratna. Whom do you admire for their commitment to the spiritual journey and/or social causes? Find out more about what they said and did by reading books by or about them, watching movies or television specials about their lives, or listening to speeches they gave.

6. Do some of your own personal-despair work. What grieves your heart personally, communally, or globally? Express your grief nonverbally by working with clay or another art medium.

7. Brainstorm a list of people in your community who could use a helping hand. Perhaps you know an individual who is struggling, an organization looking for volunteers, or a neighborhood in need of cleanup. Remembering Macy's belief that one person can effect change no matter where he or she jumps into the system, choose one simple act you can do to make a difference. Make a pact with others to carry out that act in the next week.

8. In order to nurture compassion in your own heart, spend one day viewing all other beings as your mother in a former life (read again the story of Macy's encounter with the coolie). Afterward, reflect on how this exercise affects you and your attitude toward other people.

9. Collect information on environmental groups, such as Earth First! and Greenpeace. What issues are they raising? How are they calling attention to their cause? What is your responsibility as a caretaker of the Earth on behalf of future generations?

10. Macy calls nuclear sites "sacred places" because people journey to these sites to bear witness for future generations. What sacred places exist in the community, nation, or world? Like the sojourners who test the soil and raise signs of protest at these nuclear sites, what can those who journey to these other sacred places do to celebrate the holy ground on which they stand?

11. Reflect on the meaning of "compassion." Is it possible to care for another without doing it out of pity? Can one person act from a position of strength without making the other feel inferior? How is compassion related to empathy or love? What does compassion in action look like?

FOR FURTHER READING

Friedman, Lenore. "Tsering Everest/Joanna Macy." In *Meetings with Remarkable Women: Buddhist Teachers in America.* Boston: Shambhala, 1987.

Ingram, Catherine. "Joanna Macy." In *In the Footsteps of Gandhi: Conversations with Spiritual Social Activists.* Berkeley: Parallax Press, 1990.

Macy, Joanna. *Dharma and Development: Religion as Resource in the Sarvodaya Self-Help Movement.* West Hartford, Conn.: Kumarian Press, 1985.

——. *Mutual Causality in Buddhism and General Systems Theory: The Dharma of Natural Systems.* Albany, N.Y.: State University of New York Press, 1991.

——. *World as Lover, World as Self.* Berkeley: Parallax Press, 1991.

Notes

[1]Catherine Ingram, "Joanna Macy," in *In the Footsteps of Gandhi: Conversations with Spiritual Social Activists* (Berkeley: Parallax Press, 1990), 143.

[2]Joanna Macy, *World as Lover, World as Self* (Berkeley: Parallax Press, 1991), 119–21.

[3]Ibid., 121–23.

[4]Ibid., 25–26.

[5]Ingram, 141–42.

[6]Macy, *World as Lover, World as Self,* 29.

[7]Joanna Macy, *Dharma and Development* (West Hartford, Conn.: Kumarian Press, 1985), 91–92.

[8]Ibid., 92–93.

[9]Joanne Macy, *Mutual Causality in Buddhism and General Systems Theory* (Albany, N.Y.: State University of New York Press, 1991), 217–19.

[10]Macy, *World as Lover, World as Self,* 32–33.

[11]Ibid., 220–21.

Chapter Nine

Rabindranath Tagore

Looking at the World
with an Artist's Eyes

Prepare to Meditate

*Choose a poem to be your companion for this time of meditation
and preparation. It can be a passage from the Bible (such as Psalms,
Song of Solomon, or Isaiah), the lyrics of an inspiring song, or some
verses of a favorite poem. Sit comfortably. Light a candle or burn
incense to mark this as sacred time. Slowly read the words you have
chosen. Read them over many times. Allow the beauty of the words
and the power of the images to move you deeply. Imagine yourself
living in the poem. Do not analyze what is happening, but simply
enjoy the experience of living in the world created by the poem itself.
End your meditation with thanksgiving for the one who wrote the
poem, for the poem itself, and for the gift of human imagination.*

Hear the Stories

Bengali poet and mystic Rabrindranath Tagore was fond of
retelling the ancient Buddhist story of Upagupta: Late one night
the Buddhist monk Upagupta lay sleeping beside the city wall.
Suddenly, he was awakened by the presence of a beautiful dancing girl who invited the monk to sleep in her bed. With great
compassion Upagupta rejected her offer, but promised he would
join her when the time was right. Some time later, the monk
was walking beside the city wall when he noticed a woman
lying on the ground, her body covered with sores. As he gave

her a drink and rubbed salve on her sores, he recognized her as the dancing girl who had greeted him some time before. "Who are you?" she asked. Upagupta replied, "The time has come to visit you, and I am here."[1]

This was one of Tagore's favorite stories. Perhaps he felt an affinity to the misunderstood Upagupta. Without a doubt, Tagore, who was so influential in introducing the best of Indian culture to the West and vice versa, was often misunderstood and even rejected by the people of his own country. Although he was embraced by devoted fans worldwide, Tagore's recognition at home would not come until the end of his eighty years.

Born in Calcutta in 1861, Tagore was the youngest of fourteen children and the son of the Maharishi Devendranath Tagore, a great religious reformer in India who traveled so extensively that he was rarely at home. Sarada Devi was his devoted and loving mother, whose health suffered after the birth of their fifteenth child, who died in infancy. The wealthy family lived on a luxurious estate, filled to the brim with their children, their children's spouses, and grandchildren. In this rich and active environment, eight-year-old Rabi (as he was affectionately called by his family) began writing verses and songs and found it so fulfilling that he filled many small books with his verses.

When Rabi was eleven, his father returned from one of his journeys to preside over the *upanayana*, or investiture, of his three sons. The Tagores were Hindus in the caste known as the Brahmins, "the twice born," which required that at a certain age the sons be invested with the sacred thread and initiated into the ancient rites of their religion. The three boys' heads were shaved, gold rings were placed on their ears, and they were sent on a three-day retreat in preparation of this rite. At the ceremony, the ancient chant known as *Gayatri* was recited. In English the words are translated: "Let me contemplate the adorable splendor of Him who created the earth, the air and the starry spheres, and sends the power of comprehensions within our minds." These words had a mystical affect on Rabi; though he barely comprehended the meaning of the words at the time, the rhythm and intonation of the chant touched him deeply. Throughout the rest of his life, whenever he needed to find a place of peace within himself, Tagore would recite the words of the *Gayatri*, drawing both strength and joy from this ancient chant.[2]

As a student, Rabi learned Bengali, Sanskrit, and English. He enjoyed reading classical Western works and all sorts of English and European literature. He also continued to write poetry and began to write songs. Although he attended Catholic parochial school and was tutored extensively by scholars in many different academic fields, he disliked school so much that at the age of fourteen he quit. How ironic that this man, who would eventually have such an influence on education in India, would lack academic credentials!

Rabi's family, particularly his father, did not know what to make of him. Obviously, he was a gifted poet and musician—actually a creative genius—but he seemed to have no direction in life. After he dropped out of school, his father sent him to England twice in the hope that Rabi would return with an academic degree or some training that would prepare him for a career. Both times Rabi returned empty-handed, except for the poems, novels, and songs he had written.

Through his poetry and music Tagore had begun to introduce changes that would have a huge impact on these art forms. Traditionally there were two styles in which poetry and music were written: the classical style, which was supported by centuries of discipline and direction, and the traditional religious and folk style, which appealed more to popular tastes. Tagore was the first to draw freely from both styles, using whatever suited his needs at the time. He also borrowed liberally from Western sources, giving even Western poetic forms a distinctive Eastern flair. Throughout his life he experimented with many types of writing—novels, plays, short stories, as well as poetry and songs.

When Tagore was eighteen years old, he was visiting his brother and sister-in-law during one of his many vacations at a villa on the river Ganges. It was there that he had what he called his first experience of spiritual reality. He writes: "One day while I stood watching at early dawn, the sun sending out its rays from behind the trees, I suddenly felt as if some ancient mist had in a moment lifted from my sight, and the morning light on the face of the world revealed an inner radiance of joy." This encounter had such a profound effect on him that for four days he lived in a state of heightened awareness, in which each small thing in the world was infused with joy and meaning—a man and woman walking together, a mother playing with her child and two cows standing together became beautiful images of the divine presence in the world.³ Many mark this event as Tagore's entrance into adulthood, distinguished by a new maturity in his writing.

In 1883, his family arranged his marriage to Mrinalini Devi, a young maid who worked on the Tagore estate. Throughout their marriage, she remained a supportive wife, able to create a stable climate in which his artistic genius could continue to flourish. She gave birth to three daughters and two sons.

Prior to this time in his life, Tagore had taken little interest in organized religion. Delighted that his son was now a family man, the maharishi appointed his son secretary of the Hindu reformist religious society he had founded. Always admiring his father and his work, Tagore involved himself in his new activities with much enthusiasm. He wrote hymns for congregational singing and wrote articles explaining his father's faith stance. Despite these activities, Tagore's interest in religion was never limited to Hinduism, but instead embraced all of spiritual reality. He was particularly drawn to the life and teachings of the Buddha, fascinated by the interesting mix of intellectual fervor and deep compassion for others that characterized the historical Buddha. Interestingly enough, these very same qualities have been used to describe the personality of Tagore as well.

Tagore's father was insistent that his son assume his responsibility as the member of a large, landowning family. Thus, in 1891 Rabi went to manage his father's estates in Shilaidah and Saiyadpur, in what is today part of Bangladesh, often living on a houseboat on the river Ganges. The beautiful countryside provided even more inspiration for his writing. Also, living among the poor village folk sparked his interest in social and political problems. He watched how these common people struggled daily against the uncooperative forces of nature. Their lives were made even worse by the social, economic, and political structures that treated them with indifference and conspired to keep them poor. Although he was an aristocrat by birth and upbringing, he did not turn away from the poor in disgust. Instead, he looked on them with compassion, viewing all people as children of the one Creator.

At that time, India was under the rule of the British Empire. Although the English and wealthy Indians lived well, the vast majority of Indians struggled to earn just the basic necessities of life. Tagore believed very strongly that it was wrong for people to labor so hard and to have nothing more to look forward to than continued poverty and hardship. Thus, nearly twenty years before Gandhi undertook his reform campaign, Tagore began his program of community development based on the two principles of self-help and education in the ways of science. His very first efforts in this area took place on his family estates. Later, he founded a school named Visva-Bharati at Santiniketan that offered training in large-scale community development. The peasants, he believed, lacked an understanding of how technology could be applied to their everyday lives, while the scholars had no conception whatsoever of the suffering that the poor endured daily. In all his educational efforts, he sought to build up a relationship between the learned scholars and the humble peasants so that each could benefit from the other's knowledge and experience.

Tagore was to give the rest of his life, over fifty years, to this effort on behalf of the poor. He found himself being pulled in this direction not merely out of an intellectual concern for the peasants, but as a result of his quest for spiritual truth as well. One day in particular, a day that had begun like any other day, he was preparing to take his morning bath when he paused to look out his window. The first rain of the season was beginning to fall on the marketplace that had been erected by the bank of a dry riverbed. Without warning, he became aware of a "stirring of soul" within himself. Thoughts and perceptions that were once disconnected gave way to a sense of wholeness. He described himself as being like a man who, groping around in the fog and believing himself to be hopelessly lost, discovers to his relief that he is standing in front of his own house. This "unity of vision" led him to recognize the presence of God in all of creation, human and nonhuman. He also recognized in this awareness a calling to give himself fully and completely to God, in loving cooperation with others.[4]

As the nineteenth century drew to a close, the nationalist movement in India was gaining momentum as Indians sought independence from British rule. In response to protests and strikes, Great Britain passed the Sedition Act of 1898 and arrested key leaders in the nationalist movement. Tagore used this opportunity to write and speak out in opposition to the government's oppressive activities. In the coming years, however, he became disillusioned with the nationalist movement as he watched the struggle become increasingly violent. Although he took a less public role in the movement, he continued to shape its philosophy, particularly the emphasis on nonviolence advocated by Gandhi, through articles and poetry devoted to social and political themes.

Feeling overwhelmed by the frenzy of city life, Tagore moved his family to the quiet open spaces of Santiniketan. There he founded an experimental school, Visva-Bharati, in 1901 that sought to blend the best of Eastern and Western traditions. Never forgetting his own negative experiences with the school of his childhood, he envisioned a learning environment in which teachers and students worked together and learned about both intellectual and practical matters. Rather than merely recreating the European system of education so prevalent in India, he would develop a creative system of teaching and learning that made education both meaningful and fun. Believing that nature is the best teacher, Tagore insisted that the school educate the whole person, the emotions and five senses, as well as the intellect.

Tagore's theories were not well-received by the orthodox educators and religious people of his day. His school struggled financially. He was forced to sell personal property, and his wife gladly parted with the family jewelry in order to keep the enterprise going. Because of his progressive social and religious views, he was also considered suspect by the government authorities. Secret letters were sent to government officials warning them not to send their children to Tagore's school. Tagore found that he had to rely on his own inner strength and faith in God to cope with the challenges and inevitable disappointments of cutting a new path, educationally, socially, and religiously. The first years of the twentieth century were also a time of deep personal tragedy for Tagore: between 1902 and 1907, Tagore endured the deaths of his wife, his father, a daughter, and a son.

Some of Tagore's best poetry came out of these years of intense sadness, however. In fact, he won the Nobel Prize for Literature in 1913 in recognition of his *Gitanjali*, or "Song Offering," a collection of religious poetry developed out of his loneliness and deep suffering. He was the first Asian to ever receive the

Nobel Prize for poetry. He gave a portion of the prize money to the Santiniketan school and used the rest to finance a cooperative agricultural bank to benefit the peasants living and working on the family estate.

Winning the Nobel Prize brought Tagore worldwide recognition. Increased interest in his educational theories and methods made it possible for him to expand his school so that it became a university where East met West. Called Viva-Bharati, or "universal world of knowledge and wisdom," it was based on the premise that truth takes many different forms. Accordingly, students came to the university from throughout the world. As a result of his spreading fame, Tagore was also knighted by the British government in 1915, but he angrily relinquished his knighthood in response to a massacre of Indian citizens by British soldiers in 1919. In a letter to the viceroy, Lord Chelmsford, he wrote: "The very least I can do is to take all consequences upon myself in giving voice to the protest of the millions of my countrymen...I for my part wish to stand, shorn of all special distinctions, by the side of those of my countrymen who for their so-called insignificance are liable to suffer a degradation not fit for human blessings."[5]

Tagore spent the last twenty-five years of his life traveling and writing. Although he often spoke out against the dangers of materialism, he found himself in the awkward position of having to solicit benefactors for funds to support his university. He was recognized as a man deeply devoted to the spiritual life by people all over the world. Thus, he was frequently invited to lecture in Europe, the Americas, China, Japan, Malaysia, and Indonesia. His concern for social issues, however, was always deeply entwined with his emphasis on spirituality. For example, while touring the United States and Japan in 1916 during the First World War, he regularly called for peace among the nations, stressing that peace can only be achieved through intellectual cooperation among people of goodwill.

Tagore remained quite active well into his seventies—writing, staging his plays to raise money for his schools, lecturing, and visiting world leaders at home and in distant locales. His health began to fail only in the last year of his life when, in 1941, he died one week after having surgery. He was eighty years old. In the years since his death he has been remembered as a visionary whose poetic dreams of unity and inspiring words of hope continue to touch the minds and hearts of gentle souls everywhere.

READ THE WORDS

As you read the works that follow, ask yourself these questions: What are some ways in which Tagore's writings connect to his life story? How do these words nurture my spiritual life and/or inspire me to engage in acts of social justice?

READING ONE:

Tagore won the Nobel Prize for Literature in 1913 in recognition of his book of poetry entitled Gitanjali, *which means "Song Offering."* Gitanjali *is judged by many to be the finest religious poetry he ever wrote. It was written during a time of intense suffering for the poet after he had endured the deaths of his wife, father, and two children. The three portions that follow demonstrate the lyrical quality and utter simplicity of Tagore's poetry.*

IV

Life of my life, I shall ever try to keep my body pure, knowing that thy living touch is upon all my limbs.

I shall ever try to keep all untruths out from my thoughts, knowing that thou art that truth which has kindled the light of reason in my mind.

I shall ever try to drive all evils away from my heart and keep my love in flower, knowing that thou hast thy seat in the inmost shrine of my heart.

And it shall be my endeavor to reveal thee in my actions, knowing it is thy power gives me strength to act.

XXXVI

This is my prayer to thee, my lord—strike, strike at the root of penury in my heart.

Give me the strength lightly to bear my joys and sorrows.

Give me the strength to make my love fruitful in service.

Give me the strength never to disown the poor or bend my knee before insolent might.

Give me the strength to raise my mind above daily trifles.

And give me the strength to surrender my strength to thy will with love.

<h1 style="text-align:center">CI</h1>

Ever in my life have I sought thee with my songs. It was they who led me from door to door, and with them have I felt about me, searching and touching my world.

It was my songs that taught me all the lessons I ever learnt; they showed me secret paths, they brought before my sight many a star on the horizon of my heart.

They guided me all the day long to the mysteries of the country of pleasure and pain, and at last, to what palace gate have they brought me in the evening at the end of my journey?[6]

READING TWO:

"The Cabuliwallah" (The Fruitseller from Cabul) is a short story written by Tagore in 1892. He tells the story of a special friendship between a five-year-old Indian girl named Mini and a poor peddler named Rahmun, who visits her home each day. The peddler has lived apart from his family for many years and sees in young Mini the daughter he left behind in his native Afghanistan. After an unfortunate incident, the peddler is arrested and taken away to jail. When he is released eight years later, he returns to Mini's home, only to find that she is now an adult and preparing to be married. On that day, Rahmun's encounter with Mini's father brings insight to them both.

...[Rahmun said]: "May I not see the little one, sir, for a moment?" It was his belief that Mini was still the same. He had pictured her running to him as she used to do, calling "O Cabuliwallah! Cabuliwallah!" He had imagined that they would laugh and talk together, just as in the past. In fact, in memory of those former days he had brought, carefully wrapped up in paper, a few almonds and raisins and grapes, somehow obtained from a countryman—his own little fund was gone.

I said again: "There is a ceremony in the house, and you will not be able to see any one today."

The man's face fell. He looked wistfully at me for a moment, said, "Good morning," and went out.

I felt a little sorry, and would have called him back, but saw that he was returning of his own accord. He came close up to me holding out his offerings, and said: "I brought these few things, sir, for the little one. Will you give them to her?"

I took them and was going to pay him, but he caught my hand and said: "You are very kind, sir! Keep me in your recollection; do not offer me money! You have a little girl; I too have one like her in my own home. I thought of my own, and brought fruits to your child, not to make a profit for myself."

Saying this, he put his hand inside his big loose robe and brought out a small dirty piece of paper. With great care he unfolded this, and smoothed it out with both hands on my table. It bore the impression of a little hand, not a photograph, not a drawing. The impression of an ink-smeared hand laid flat on the paper. This touch of his own little daughter had been always on his heart, as he had come year after year to Calcutta to sell his wares in the streets.

Tears came to my eyes. I forgot that he was a poor Cabuli fruit-seller, while I was—but no, was I more than he? He was also a father.

That impression of the hand of his little Parbati in her distant mountain home reminded me of my own little Mini, and I immediately sent for her in the inner apartment...The Cabuliwallah was staggered at the sight of her. There was no hope of reviving their old friendship...

I remembered the day when the Cabuliwallah and my Mini first met, and I felt sad. When she had gone, Rahmun heaved a deep sigh and sat down on the floor. The idea had suddenly come to him that his daughter also must have grown up during this long time, and that he would have to make friends with her all over again. Surely he would not find her as he used to know her; besides, what might have happened to her in these eight years.

The marriage-pipes sounded, and the mild autumn sun streamed around us. But Rahmun sat in the little Calcutta lane, and saw before him the barren mountains of Afghanistan.

I took out a bank-note and gave it to him, saying: "Go back to your own daughter, Rahmun, in your own country, and may the happiness of your meeting bring good fortune to my child!"

After giving this gift, I had to eliminate some of the festivities. I could not have the electric lights, nor the military band, and the ladies of the house were saddened. But to me the wedding-feast was brighter because of the thought that in a distant land a long-lost father met again with his only child.[7]

READING THREE:
Tagore's efforts in education, though challenged at first, brought about major changes in the way that students were educated in India. He was the first to introduce a curriculum that combined the best of Eastern and Western influences, including the knowledge that can be found both in books and in nature. In this excerpt from a series of talks he gave in China in 1924, he discusses how his own early educational experiences led him to take on this huge task.

When I was very young I gave up learning and ran away from my lessons. That saved me, and I owe all I possess today to that courageous step. I fled the classes which instructed, but which did not inspire me, and I gained a sensitivity toward life and nature.

It is a great world to which we have been born, and if I had cultivated a callous mind, and smothered this sensitivity under a pile of books, I would have lost this world. We can ignore what is scattered in the blue sky, in the seasonal flowers, in the delicate relationships of love and sympathy and mutual friendship only if we have deadened the thrill of touching the reality which is everywhere—in man, in nature, in everything. I kept this sensitiveness.

If mother Nature could do it, she would bless and kiss me, and would say, "You have loved me." I have lived not as a member of a society or group, but as a scamp and a vagabond, free in a world which I have seen face to face. I have experienced the mystery of its being: its heart and soul. You may call me uneducated and uncultured, just a foolish poet; you may become great scholars and philosophers; and yet I think I would still retain the right to laugh at pedantic scholarship.

I know, really, that you do not dislike me because I know less mathematics than you; for you believe that I have attained the secret of existence in some other way—not through analysis, but as a child who enters his mother's chamber. I have kept the child spirit, and have found entrance to my mother's chamber; it was from her that the symphony of awakening light sang to me from the distant horizon, and I sing now in response to it.[8]

READING FOUR:

The love poems in The Gardener, *published in 1913, are some of the most beautiful compositions Tagore ever wrote. This tale of two birds expresses the longing of a love that cannot be fulfilled because irreconcilable differences keep the two lovers apart.*

> The tame bird was in a cage, the free bird was in the
>   forest.
> They met when the time came, it was a decree of fate.
> The free bird cries, "O my love, let us fly to the wood."
> The cage bird whispers, "Come hither, let us both live in
>   the cage."
> Says the free bird, "Among bars, where is there room to
>   spread one's wings?"
> "Alas," cries the cage bird, "I should not know where to
>   sit perched in the sky."
>
> The free bird cries, "My darling, sing the songs of the
>   woodlands."
> The cage bird says, "Sit by my side, I'll teach you the
>   speech of the learned."
> The forest bird cries, "No, ah no! songs can never be
>   taught."
> The cage bird says, "Alas for me, I know not the songs of
>   the woodlands."
>
> Their love is intense with longing, but they never fly
>   wing to wing.
> Through bars of the cage they look, and vain is their
>   wish to know each other.
> They flutter their wings in yearning, and sing,
>   "Come closer, my love!"
> The free bird cries, "It cannot be, I fear the closed doors
>   of the cage."
> The cage bird whispers, "Alas, my wings are powerless
>   and dead."[9]

READING FIVE:

The Religion of Man *is a collection of lectures Tagore delivered in 1930 at Oxford, England. These writings provide a fascinating glimpse into the artist's understanding of creativity and the spiritual quest. Here Tagore discusses the religious meaning he finds in the natural world.*

From my infancy I had a keen sensitivity which kept my mind tingling with consciousness of the world around me, natural and human. We had a small garden attached to our house; it was a fairyland for me, where miracles of beauty were of everyday occurrence.

Almost every morning in the early hour of the dusk, I would run out from my bed in a great hurry to greet the first pink flush of the dawn through the shivering branches of the palm trees which stood in a line along the garden boundary, while the grass glistened as the dew-drops caught the earliest tremor of the morning breeze. The sky seemed to bring to me the call of a personal companionship, and all my heart—my whole body in fact—used to drink in at a draught the overflowing light and peace of those silent hours. I was anxious never to miss a single morning, because each one was precious to me, more precious than gold to the miser. I am certain that I felt a larger meaning of my own self when the barrier vanished between me and what was beyond myself.

I had been blessed with that sense of wonder which gives a child his right of entry into the treasure house of mystery in the depth of existence. My studies in the school I neglected, because they rudely dismembered me from the context of my world and I felt miserable, like a caged rabbit in a biological institute. This, perhaps, will explain the meaning of my religion. This world was living to me, intimately close to my life, permeated by a subtle touch of kinship which enhanced the value of my own being...

I still remember the shock of repulsion I received as a child when some medical student brought to me a piece of the human windpipe and tried to excite my admiration for its structure. He tried to convince me that it was the source of the beautiful human voice. But I could not bear the artisan to occupy the throne that was for the artist who concealed the machinery and revealed the creation in its ineffable unity. God does not care to keep exposed the record of his power written in geological inscriptions, but he is proudly glad of the expression of beauty which he spreads on the green grass, in the flowers, in the play of the colors on the clouds, in the murmuring music of running water.[10]

Reflect and Act

By yourself, or in cooperation with others, engage in the following reflection and action exercises. Try to do one exercise each day for a week. If one activity is particularly meaningful, stay with it for a longer period of time. Also feel free to create exercises of your own as you are inspired by the life and witness of Rabindranath Tagore.

1. Think of a story, either fictional or true, that has been especially meaningful to you and has provided inspiration for your life journey. Take some time to reflect on its meaning for your life, then invite the members of the group to share their stories with one another. What makes these stories special and different somehow from all the other stories that make up our lives?

2. What struggles and hardships exist within your own local community? Who is involved in these struggles—people, animals, the environment, others? Choose one issue that is of special interest to you. Brainstorm concrete actions you could take to express your solidarity with those who struggle. The actions could be as simple as writing a letter, or as complex as mounting a campaign. Pick one of these actions and carry it out in the next week.

3. Create a book of poetry, made up of compositions you have written yourself, poems others have written, or a combination of both. For each poem, reflect on why it has meaning for you by writing a short response or drawing a picture. Try to engage each poem by reflecting not only on what it *means* to you, but also on how it makes you *feel* and what it *moves* you to do and be.

4. Tagore sought to bring scholars and peasants together for discussions, believing that each could benefit from the wisdom and experience of the other. What different groups in

today's society could benefit from talking to each other? What would they talk about? What issues would be important to each of them? In cooperation with others, role-play a discussion between two groups in society. Allow the group members to choose what role they will play.

5. Reflect on your formal educational experiences, such as elementary, junior high and senior high school, college classes, community learning courses, or Sunday school classes. Which were the most meaningful for you? Least meaningful? What contributed to their meaning for you? Write about your experiences in your journal or discuss them with a friend.

6. Early in this century Tagore was knighted by the British government, but angrily renounced his knighthood when a group of Indian protesters were killed by British soldiers. When have you been moved to speak out against injustice? For what issues would you participate in a protest? How much would you be willing to sacrifice for what you believe to be right? Consider if there are issues for which you could raise your voice or lend your hand today. Gather information this week by making phone calls, going to the library, writing some letters, or searching the Internet. Make a decision about your involvement in this cause.

7. In Reading Three, Tagore talks of his "child spirit," which enabled him to look at the world with a sense of novelty and wonder. Where do you see this child spirit in yourself and others? Try to engage your child spirit by participating in a some playful activity, such as drawing with crayons, swinging at a playground, playing make-believe, or building with blocks. Explore ways to invite your child spirit to be a trusted and welcome companion in your daily life.

8. The beautiful poetry of *Gitanjali* was composed during a time of intense suffering for Tagore. What is it about hardship that makes it fertile ground for creativity? Can you think of similar situations from your life or the lives of others? Think about the ways in which artistic endeavors can ease the pain of suffering for yourself or others.

9. Choose a word or phrase to describe the way you and those around you relate to the natural world. Are you satisfied

with your current relationship with nature, or do you want to make some changes? What would those changes be, and how would you enact them? Express your feelings by singing a song, creating a poster, composing a poem, or writing a letter. Do you think that an appreciation for the natural world can enhance spiritual wholeness?

10. Imagine a world in which there were no poets, artists, or musicians. How would you describe such a world? What would be gained if they did not exist? What would be lost without them? Where does the artistic exist within you? What impact does it have on your life?

For Further Reading

Kripalani, Krishna. *Rabindranath Tagore: A Biography.* New York: Grove Press, 1962.

Lago, Mary M. *Rabindranath Tagore.* Boston: Twayne, 1976.

Tagore, Rabindranath. *The Hungry Stones and Other Stories.* New York: The Macmillan Company, 1916.

——. *The Religion of Man.* Boston: Beacon Press, 1931.

——. *A Tagore Reader.* Edited by Amiya Chakravarty. New York: The Macmillan Company, 1961.

——. *Collected Poems and Plays of Rabindranath Tagore.* New York: Macmillan Publishing, 1977.

Notes

[1] Rabrindranath Tagore, *Collected Poems and Plays of Rabindranath Tagore* (New York: Macmillan Publishing, 1977), 154–55.

[2] Krishna Kripalani, *Rabindranath Tagore: A Biography* (New York: Grove Press, 1962), 47–48.

[3] Rabindranath Tagore, *The Religion of Man* (Boston: Beacon Press, 1931), 93–94.

[4] Ibid., 94–96.

[5] Kripalani, 266.

[6] Tagore, *Collected Poems and Plays*, 4, 13–14, and 37.

[7] Rabindranath Tagore, *A Tagore Reader*, ed. Amiya Chakravarty (New York: The Macmillan Company, 1961), 46–53.

[8] Ibid., 206–7.

[9] Tagore, *Collected Poems and Plays*, 77.

[10] Tagore, *The Religion of Man*, 98–99 and 100–101.

Chapter Ten

Dorothy Day

Seeing Christ
in the Faces of the Poor

PREPARE TO MEDITATE

Prepare to meditate by closing your eyes, sitting in a comfortable position, lighting a candle, listening to soft music, or doing any other activity that is meaningful for you. Choose one troubling aspect of modern life, such as a particular war, the suffering of the poor, borrowing and lending, domestic violence, or the disillusionment and despair of young people. Meditate on the world as it is today with regard to that particular issue. In your mind's eye see the people who are affected, feel their joy and pain, and experience the world as they do. Do this without rational analysis or commentary; focus instead on how this exercise feels in heart, body, and soul. Then, envision the world as it could be, a world where suffering is eased and pain is relieved. How is God pulling the world toward that ideal vision? Do you see people who are moved to catch the vision and act on it?

HEAR THE STORIES

In her autobiography, *The Long Loneliness*, Dorothy Day asks a poignant question: "The problem is, how to love God?"[1] This, in fact, has been the main question that has guided much of Day's life. Her struggle to love God has led her to forsake physical comforts, to risk the misunderstanding of family and friends,

145

and to turn toward the care of the suffering, often at great personal sacrifice.

Day's story began in 1897 when she was born in Brooklyn Heights, New York, in a home not far from the Brooklyn Bridge. She was the third of five children born to Grace Satterlee and John Day. John was a newspaperman who specialized in horse racing and whose frequent job changes caused the Day family to move often. The first such move was to Oakland, California, in 1904 when John accepted a job to cover the races at a horse track near there. Grace was a devoted wife and mother who provided stability for the family amid occasional poverty and uncertainty.

One of Day's earliest religious memories occurred at their home in Oakland. One day, while playing in the attic, she came upon a musty Bible. She read it for hours, sensing its holiness, but unaware of what she was reading. She also began to go to church, pray, and sing hymns with the Methodist family who lived next door. She became, she says, "disgustingly, proudly pious." When she asked her mother why their family did not do these things, she did not receive a satisfactory answer. Although she was the only one to do so, she continued to go to church.[2]

Tragically, a severe earthquake in San Francisco in 1906 caused the building housing the printing press of the newspaper for which John worked to burn to the ground. Out of work, the family sold what was left of their personal property and moved to Chicago. There they rented a dilapidated six-room tenement flat over a tavern, just two blocks from Lake Michigan. The children were so embarrassed by their accommodations that they would pretend they lived elsewhere by walking into another, more impressive building when they knew others were watching. When John did get a job as sports editor of a local paper, the family was able to move to a large house on Chicago's North Side.

Day had several encounters with religion during her childhood in the city. She particularly remembers a good friend in the tenements, Mary Harrington, who used to tell her about the saints. She also recalls the time she entered the flats looking for another one of her friends. She ran from room to room hoping to find Kathryn, but instead came upon her mother, Mrs. Barrett, on her knees, saying her prayers. Mrs. Barrett paused just a moment to tell Dorothy that Kathryn had gone to the store, and then she resumed her praying. Day calls this her "first impulse toward Catholicism."[3] Soon after, she began to attend the local Episcopal Church. She was especially touched by the words of the *Benedicite:* "All ye works of the Lord, bless ye the Lord, praise Him and magnify Him forever."

By the age of ten Day had become a voracious reader, reading the classic works of Victor Hugo, Charles Dickens, Robert Louis Stevenson, and Edgar Allan Poe. Indeed, her love of books remained with her throughout her lifetime. By the time she was a senior in high school, however, she had begun to read the works of radical socialist writers and activists. The book that was most influential for Day during this time was Upton Sinclair's *The Jungle,* a fictional account of the horrid conditions under which immigrants labored in Chicago's stockyards and slaughterhouses early this century. From then on, rather than sit in Lincoln Park or walk along the beachfront each evening, Day began to take long walks toward the West Side of Chicago, where she could see firsthand the places the poor lived and worked. She was surprised, not only by the squalor of the surroundings but also by the glimpses of beauty—small vegetable gardens ringed by bright marigolds, the smell of lumber and coffee, and the scent of bread and coffee cake. Although others might see the poor as worthless and responsible for their own well-being, Day decided "that from then on my life was to be linked to theirs, their interests were to be mine: I had received a call, a vocation, a direction in my life."[4]

Day found herself growing more disillusioned with the church. She was angry that the church was doing so little to meet the needs of the poor and instead was concerned only with the rich. These concerns continued when she went away to college at the University of Illinois in Urbana. She immersed herself ever more deeply in the writings and speeches of socialists. Again and again she asked why society worked to alleviate the sufferings of people without ever tackling the underlying causes of those problems.

At eighteen, having completed just two years of college, Day moved with her parents to New York where her father began work with another newspaper. Knowing that she needed a job and a place of her own, she made the rounds of the newspapers, but kept encountering editors who told her that a woman didn't belong in the newspaper business. It took five months before she walked into the office of *The Call*, a socialist daily. The editor, Chester Wright, had no problem with hiring a woman writer, but had no money to pay her. In a moment of inspiration, she told him that she had heard of police officers who had formed "diet squads," groups committed to feeding themselves on five dollars a week as proof that the poor could make it on as little as that. If *The Call* could pay her five dollars a week, she would live on a limited budget and write about it for the newspaper. Wright was so taken with the idea that he agreed to hire Day for five dollars a week for the first month with the promise of raising her salary to twelve dollars a week after that. Rising to meet her own challenge, Day fed herself on twenty-five cents a day and lived in a vermin-infested apartment costing five dollars a month.[5]

Her work as a reporter entailed covering workers' meetings and strikes, listening to speeches, and interviewing great thinkers of the socialist movement. With the loss of her job and the coming of the Great War, however, Day found herself only twenty years old, depressed, and uncertain where to turn next. Wanting to help others in need, she trained as a nurse at Kings County Hospital in Brooklyn. This work, though difficult, filled her with joy since she was no longer observing and writing about the poor and sick, but caring for them. While there she fell in love with an orderly at the hospital, Lionel Moise. She quit her job and moved in with him. When she became pregnant, he took a job out of the country, leaving her money for an abortion. Not wanting to raise a child on her own, she had the abortion.

Soon after, she met Berkeley Tobey, a founder of the Literary Guild and one of the wealthier inhabitants of Greenwich Village. She married him on the rebound, but their marriage lasted less than a year. Trying to get her life back in order, she took a job with the City News Bureau and roomed with three women in a Catholic household. For the first time in her life, she witnessed the depth of religious practice and spirituality as exemplified by these women. Through their devotion to weekly mass, daily prayer, and moral purity, she had a model for the Christian life that she wanted to follow.

Having come into a substantial amount of money by selling a screenplay to Hollywood producers, she bought a fisherman's cottage on the beach on Staten Island in the 1920s. Soon after, she met a man with whom she fell in love. Forster Batterham was an anarchist who did not believe in religion or marriage. Now that Dorothy believed firmly in the existence of God, they would have bitter arguments about faith. He moved into her cottage, and they shared an intimate, loving relationship. Although they never married, Day referred to Forster as her "husband" until the end of her life.

Thus began a time of inner spirituality for Day. She had been given a rosary years earlier; now she used it to say daily prayers while walking to and from the post office in a neighboring town. When she walked along the shore looking for driftwood for the fire, she recited the words of the *Benedicite* that she had learned in the Episcopal Church of her childhood. While doing housework she would turn toward a statue of Mary, the mother of Jesus, and talk with her. Because she knew that none of her friends would understand her private devotion, she did not share her experiences with anyone.

When she discovered to Forster's dismay that she was pregnant, she was overjoyed. The one thing missing from her life was motherhood. The birth of her daughter, Tamar Teresa, in 1926, cemented Day's connection with the Roman Catholic Church. Her daughter was baptized the following year. Although it was a difficult and painful decision, Day severed her relationship with Forster later that year, so that she too could be baptized and become a member of the Catholic Church.

Throughout these early days in the church she felt a strange tension. Although she was drawn to the liturgy and spiritual dimension of the church, she agreed with many of her friends that the institutional church seemed to care very little about the poor and oppressed. Witnessing the Hunger March of 1932, however, proved to be the turning point in Day's lifelong commitment to living the spiritual life through social activism.

While the United States was in the grip of the Great Depression, six hundred unemployed marchers left New York City on their way to Washington, D.C., asking the government to provide jobs, unemployment insurance, old-age pensions, relief for

mothers and children, health care, and housing for those suffering across the nation. Because the march was sponsored by
Communists, the requests of the marchers were not taken very
seriously. Both the newspapers and the government viewed this
as an example of Communist infiltration. At one stop in
Wilmington, Delaware, for instance, the marchers were brutal-
ized with tear gas, and the leaders were thrown in jail.
Nevertheless, the group pushed on toward Washington. When
they reached the capital, it was discovered that police had barri-
caded the city, making it impossible for the marchers to enter.
Undeterred, they set up camp outside the city and stayed there
for three days. Finally, the barricades were removed, and the
jobless marched triumphantly into the city, carrying placards
and shouting slogans. Day stood on the curb watching them go
by. Her joy at their success was mixed with sorrow that she and
her church were doing nothing to help the workers. That afternoon she went to church to pray and there she asked God to
provide a way for her to use her talents on behalf of the workers
and the poor.[6]

When she returned to New York, she was greeted by a visitor, a man who introduced himself as Peter Maurin. He explained
that mutual friends had told him to seek her out, saying that the
two of them thought alike. He had been praying for a collabora-
tor and was convinced that Day was the answer to his prayer.
He invited her to participate with him in heralding a revolution,
not one built on violence, but on the Christian social teachings
of the Catholic Church. He proposed to her that they write a
publication that would tie church teaching with this new world
order. "But where do we get the money?" she asked. "God sends
you what you need when you need it," Maurin answered. "Just
read the lives of the saints." And so, with Day and Maurin writing articles, Day's brother helping with mock-up, and Day and
Tamar selling copies on the street, *The Catholic Worker* was born.[7]

The first copy of this radical, Catholic newspaper was handed
out in Union Square, New York City on May Day, 1933. They
gave a copy of the eight-page tabloid to any one who would
take it without even asking for the cover price, just one penny.
By the end of the year, the number of copies being printed rose
from 2,500 to 100,000, as Christian activists found a forum for
their concerns.

In addition to their editorial work, the writers of *The Catholic Worker* found themselves inundated with requests for assistance from the poor and needy. After all, the United States was in the midst of the Great Depression, with thirteen million people unemployed. With a steady stream of monetary donations coming in, they were able to rent apartments and even a house for use by writers, visitors, and the homeless. By 1936 *The Catholic Worker* had moved into two buildings in Chinatown and thirty-three other Catholic Worker hospitality houses had opened across the country. In 1937 the New York house alone was feeding four hundred people a day. From the beginning Day made it clear that all who asked for assistance would be gladly welcomed. None who came for help were preached to, nor were they forced into rehabilitation or job-training programs. She viewed everyone as members of the family, as her brothers and sisters in Christ.

Under Day's leadership, *The Catholic Worker* took a strong pacifist stand in response to U.S. involvement in the Spanish Civil War and World War II. Many subscriptions were cancelled; many Catholic Christians viewed this stance as unpatriotic and un-American. As many of the former unemployed and homeless went off to Europe to fight a war, one member of the Chicago Catholic Worker community even went so far as to say that the Catholic Worker movement was dead, having outlived its purpose and usefulness. Nevertheless, Day stood firm, continuing to write and edit the monthly journal, often including a simple drawing on the front page: St. Francis standing beside a tame wolf with the caption "Peace without victory."

About this same time, Day was feeling the need to deepen her spiritual life. Through the influence of some Catholic priests who shared her radical social views and commitment to spiritual renewal, the Catholic Worker movement began to sponsor regular retreats. These retreats came to affect every aspect of the movement, from interpersonal relationships, to the content of the newspaper, to the atmosphere of the hospitality houses. Although Day once went on a six-month retreat, she knew that she was meant to live the active, not the solitary, life.

As World War II drew to a close and the cold war began, the members of the Catholic Worker community continued to take a strong pacifist stand, often leading to protest and arrest.

For instance, beginning in 1955, New York City conducted civil defense drills in which citizens were to leave their cars, homes, and places of business and to retreat to bomb shelters beneath the city. Each year, Day and others gathered in City Hall Park, refusing to participate on the grounds that preparing for war does not lead to peace. They were routinely arrested, fined, and often put in jail. "It is good to be here, Lord," Dorothy wrote while serving a thirty-day jail sentence in 1957. "We were, frankly, hoping for jail. Then we would not be running a house of hospitality, we would not be dispensing food and clothing, we would not be ministering to the destitute, but we would be truly one of them."[8] The last drill took place in 1961, when air-raid sirens were defied by over two thousand people who stood and laughed in front of City Hall. Although forty people were arrested that day, it was only a symbolic gesture, for New York City never had another civil defense drill.

In the early 1960s Roman Catholics watched in wonder as Pope John XXIII convened the Second Vatican Council in Rome. Looking back now we know what a profound effect that council had on the Roman Catholic Church and its relationship to other churches and religious groups. At the time, Day was hopeful that the council would make a statement against war and support pacifists and advocates of nonviolence. In fact, during one of her several trips to Rome, she was part of a contingent of twenty Catholic women who met with the bishops and participated in a ten-day fast calling the council to make a clear statement: "Put away thy sword." She had fasted many times before, but this one was particularly hard on her sixty-eight-year-old body. On the day the fast ended she felt that her contribution had been so small, barely even noticed by the bishops, but she knew that prayer did have a powerful effect, even if it was hidden and behind the scenes.

Day and her friends were ecstatic to learn that in the final draft of the pastoral constitution, supported by nearly all the bishops, the council condemned acts of war as crimes against God and humanity, called on national governments to make provisions for conscientious objectors, and praised those who seek nonviolent means to bring an end to conflict. The following year Day was invited back to Rome where she was treated like an honored guest and was one of two Americans to receive communion from the hands of Pope Paul VI. When a journalist asked her how this privilege made her feel, she simply said that during the mass she prayed first for the Pope, who had been ill and was not looking well that particular morning. Then she prayed for the many young people presently in jail because they refused to fight in the "terrible" war in Vietnam.[9]

Back at home, Day actively challenged the government's role in Vietnam. She watched as her friends burned their draft cards and carried out violent acts against government property. She remained true to her conviction that nonviolent means were necessary to accomplish peaceful ends, but she supported those who acted out of the convictions of their consciences. Most Catholic bishops were supportive of the U.S. involvement in Vietnam, and Day took them to task as well, reminding them that "We are all one, all one body, Chinese, Russians, Vietnamese, and He has *commanded* us to love one another."[10] In the 1970s, Day participated in strikes and the grape boycott on behalf of United Farm Workers in California. This was the last time she was imprisoned, spending ten days on a prison work farm in 1973. She was seventy-five years old at the time.

In 1975, Day retired from her day-to-day activities with *The Catholic Worker*. She continued, however, to write her column "On Pilgrimage" for the newspaper. Her last years were quiet, though she did receive a few visitors, read many novels, and write daily in her diary. She died at home of heart failure in 1980, her daughter Tamar by her side. Through the ongoing witness of *The Catholic Worker* and the movement's hospitality homes, the legacy of Dorothy Day lives on. Perhaps greater still, however, is the inspiration her life story continues to provide today for those who seek to live out their spiritual calling through acts of mercy and love.

READ THE WORDS

As you read the works that follow, ask yourself these questions: What are some ways in which Day's writings connect to her life story? How do these words nurture my spiritual life and/or inspire me to engage in acts of social justice?

READING ONE:

Beginning with the first issue of The Catholic Worker *in 1933, and continuing until her retirement in 1975, Day wrote editorials and articles for the newspaper each month. This column, dated February 1937, is entitled "They Knew Him in the Breaking of Bread." In it, she contemplates the large number of hungry persons who come to their offices each day.*

Every morning about four hundred men come to Mott Street to be fed. The radio is cheerful, the smell of coffee is a good smell, the air of the morning is fresh and not too cold, but my heart bleeds as I pass the lines of men in front of the store which is our headquarters. The place is packed—not another man can get in—so they have to form a line. Always we have hated lines, and now the breakfast which we serve of cottage cheese and rye bread and coffee has brought about a line. It is an eyesore to the community. This little Italian village which is Mott Street and Hester Street, this little community within the great city, has been invaded by the Bowery, by the hosts of unemployed men, by no means derelicts, who are trying to keep body and soul together while they look for work. It is hard to say, matter-of-factly and cheerfully, "Good morning," as we pass on our way to Mass. It is the hardest to say "Merry Christmas" or "Happy New Year" during the holiday time, to these men with despair and patient misery written on many of their faces.

One felt more like taking their hands and saying, "Forgive us—let us forgive each other! All of us who are more comfortable, who have a place to sleep, three meals a day, work to do—we are responsible for your condition. We are guilty of each other's sins. We must bear each other's burdens. Forgive us and may God forgive us all!"[11]

READING TWO:

"Love Is the Measure" is a column from the June 1946 edition of The Catholic Worker. *When Christians have done all they are able and it is still not enough to meet all the needs, Day says, then the one thing that must continue is the Christian expression of love for those whom they serve.*

We confess to being fools and wish that we were more so. In the face of the approaching atom bomb test (and discussion of widespread radioactivity is giving people more and more of an excuse to get away from the philosophy of personalism and the doctrine of free will); in the face of an approaching maritime strike; in the face of bread shortages and housing shortages; in the face of the passing of the draft extension, teenagers included, we face the situation that there is nothing we can do for people except to love them. If the maritime strike goes on, there will be no shipping of food or medicine or clothes to Europe or the Far East, so there is nothing to do again but love. We continue in our fourteenth year of feeding our brothers and sisters, clothing them and sheltering them, and the more we do it, the more we realize that the most important thing is to love. There are several families with us, destitute families, destitute to an unbelievable extent, and there, too, is nothing to do but to love. What I mean is that there is no chance of rehabilitation, no chance, so far as we see, of changing them; certainly no chance of adjusting them to this abominable world about them—and who wants them adjusted, anyway?

What we would like to do is change the world—make it a little simpler for people to feed, clothe, and shelter themselves as God intended them to do. And to a certain extent, by fighting for better conditions, by crying out unceasingly for the rights of the workers, of the poor, of the destitute—the rights of the worthy and the unworthy poor, in other words—we can to a certain extent change the world; we can work for the oasis, the little cell of joy and peace in a harried world. We can throw our pebble in the pond and be confident that its ever-widening circle will reach around the world.

We repeat, there is nothing that we can do but love, and dear God—please enlarge our hearts to love each other, to love our neighbor, to love our enemy as well as our friend.[12]

READING THREE:

In 1963, Loaves and Fishes *was published. This book tells in more detail the story of the Catholic Worker movement, the publishing and activism in which its members engaged. This chapter contains*

Day's reflections on poverty, especially the difference between the voluntary poverty that Day and other Catholic Workers had freely chosen and the inflicted poverty that so many people are unable to escape.

A BABY IS ALWAYS BORN WITH A LOAF OF BREAD UNDER ITS ARM

This was the consoling remark my brother's Spanish mother-in-law used to make when a new baby was about to arrive. It is this philosophy which makes it possible for people to endure a life of poverty.

"Just give me a chance," I hear people say. "Just let me get my debts paid. Just let me get a few of the things I need, and then I'll begin to think of poverty and its rewards. Meanwhile, I've had nothing but." But these people do not understand the difference between inflicted poverty and voluntary poverty; between being the victims and the champions of poverty. I prefer to call the one kind *destitution*, reserving the word *poverty* for what Saint Francis called "Lady Poverty."[13]

It is hard to advocate poverty when a visitor tells you how he and his family lived in a basement room and did sweatshop work at night to make ends meet, then how the landlord came in and abused them for not paying promptly his exorbitant rent.

How can we say to such people, "Be glad and rejoice, for your reward is very great in Heaven," especially when we are living comfortably in a warm house and sitting down to a good table, and are clothed warmly?[14]

READING FOUR:

Throughout her tenure at The Catholic Worker, *Day espoused a strong pacifist stance. Accordingly, during the 1960s, she spoke out against U.S. involvement in Vietnam and supported those young men who refused to go to war. In this column, from the February 1969 edition, she describes these different forms of protest as "penance" for the ways in which all people have a hand in creating, encouraging, and ignoring the suffering that takes place throughout the world.*

Penance seems to be ruled out today. One hears the Mass described as Sacrament, not as Sacrifice. But how are we to keep our courage unless the Cross, that mighty failure, is kept in view? ...The impulse to stand out against the state and go to jail rather than serve is an instinct for penance, to take on some of the suffering of the world, to share in it.

Father Anthony Mullaney, O.S.B., who is one of the Milwaukee 14, priests and laymen who burned draft records with napalm—"burning property, not people"—told me, when I met him in Boston the other day, that over a hundred of the students at St. Anselm's in Manchester, New Hampshire, signed a petition to the court, which they are going to send when the Milwaukee 14 are sentenced, offering to divide up the months or years the fourteen have to serve, and take on the sentences for them. What is this but an offer to do penance, another example of trying to follow in the steps of Christ, who took on Himself our sins and in so doing overcame both sin and death?...

The thing is to recognize that not all are called, not all have the vocation, to demonstrate in this way, to fast, to endure the pain and long-drawn-out nerve-racking suffering of prison life. We do what we can, and the whole field of all the Works of Mercy is open to us. There is a saying, "Do what you are doing." If you are a student, study, prepare, in order to give to others, and keep alive in yourself the vision of a new social order. All work, whether building, increasing food production, running credit unions, working in factories which produce for human needs, working the smallest of industries, the handicrafts—all these things can come under the heading of the Works of Mercy, which are the opposite of the works of war...

So let us rejoice in our own petty sufferings and thank God we have a little penance to offer, in this holy season. "An injury to one is an injury to all," the Industrial Workers of the World proclaimed. So an act of love, a voluntary taking on oneself of some of the pain of the world, increases the courage and love and hope of all.[15]

REFLECT AND ACT

By yourself, or in cooperation with others, engage in the following reflection and action exercises. Try to do one exercise each day for a week. If one activity is particularly meaningful, stay with it for a longer period of time. Also feel free to create exercises of your own as you are inspired by the life and witness of Dorothy Day.

1. Day's awareness of a call to serve the poor occurred earlier than her awareness that she was called to serve God, though the two callings seem to be intricately linked. Where do you see God active in calling Day toward her vocation even in the early days of her life, before she professed belief in God? How were Day's socialist leanings and activist impulses preparation for the work God would have her do later?

2. Think over the past month and remember the books, television programs, and movies you read or watched. How did these media affect you spiritually, in both positive and negatives ways? Silently ponder the emotions you felt, those things you learned, and the challenges presented to you as a result of your encounter with these forms of entertainment. Consider how you might receive greater spiritual satisfaction from these experiences.

3. Reflect on the difference between caring *about* the poor and sick, and physically caring *for* them. Remember a time when you did one or the other or both. What is the difference in perspective between caring about and caring for? How does each affect your perception of yourself and those for whom you are caring?

4. Imagine that the year is 1933. You are an unemployed man in New York City, having lost your job as a result of this country's economic depression. You feel the responsibility of providing for a wife and two children. You do not know how much longer you will be allowed to stay in the two-bedroom tenement apartment in which your family lives. One day, you come across the breadline at the Catholic Worker described by Day in the first reading above. How do you feel about yourself and your life? What are the men saying to one another in the breadline? How are you treated when you get inside the building for breakfast? Express the depth of your imaginative experience by writing a short play about what transpired that day, a letter to a relative in another city recounting your day, or a poem describing your feelings.

5. One of the more controversial aspects of Day's ministry was her refusal to force the hungry to listen to sermons or to

enter treatment and job training programs. Instead, she offered help to all who requested it, not making a distinction
between the "worthy" and the "unworthy" poor. Why do
you suppose she believed and acted this way? Search her
life story and writings for answers to this question. If possible, research information on how effective rehabilitation
and educational programs are in alleviating poverty.

6. Day's spiritual awareness led her to do penance and to seek
forgiveness for the suffering of others, which she likened to
the sacrificial death of Jesus Christ on behalf of the sins of
the entire world. She believed that those who have a warm
place to sleep, clean clothes to wear, and food to eat have a
responsibility not only to assist those who do not have those
things but to seek their forgiveness as well. What does it
mean to do penance for the suffering of others? What would
be the result if people cared for each other in this radical
way? How would you do penance or seek forgiveness if you
felt called to do so?

7. Consider Day's comparison of voluntary poverty and inflicted
poverty described in Reading Three. On a chalkboard or
piece of paper, list the characteristics of each. Include not
only the physical aspects of each poverty but the emotional,
spiritual, and psychological dimensions as well. Look at Day's
life for examples of both types of poverty. Look at your community, nation, and world for both of them as well. What
would it mean for you, your family, or your community to
embrace voluntary poverty as a way of life? If you feel led,
make the commitment to make one change in your life this
week that would take you in that direction.

8. In 1932, Day prayed for God to allow her to use her gifts to
serve the poor. Within a week, she met Peter Maurin and
the Catholic Worker movement was begun. Using an artistic
medium, such as painting, drawing, dancing, writing, or
singing, rejoice in a prayer that was answered in your lifetime.
What was your attitude while offering this prayer—receptive,
expectant, tentative, confident? Was the answer what you
expected? How did this prayer and its answer affect you
spiritually and in other ways?

9. A metaphor that Day often used to describe her work was that of a pebble being dropped into water—one simple action creates a ripple effect that reaches all the way to the water's edge. She writes that just as one injury causes many to suffer, so too can one act of goodwill bring joy and relief to many. How have you seen this to be true? What limitations are there on helping others? Recount for yourself or others an example from your life when a small act had larger consequences than you expected.

10. In the third reading, Day has described heaven as a banquet at which all who are hungry are filled. As you think about the different needs, desires, and hopes the people might express in this world (including your own), what other images of heaven can you uncover? Choose one image that is particularly meaningful for you and, in a state of silent prayer, meditate on it for ten to fifteen minutes. What sights, sounds, and emotions does it conjure up for you?

For Further Reading

Coles, Robert. *Dorothy Day: A Radical Devotion.* New York: Perseus Books, 1987.

Day, Dorothy. *The Long Loneliness.* San Francisco: HarperCollins, 1952.

————. *Loaves and Fishes.* New York: Harper and Row, 1963.

————. *Dorothy Day: Selected Writings: By Little and By Little.* Edited by Robert Ellsberg and Tamar Hennessey. Maryknoll, N.Y.: Orbis Books, 1992.

Forest, Jim. *Love Is the Measure: A Biography of Dorothy Day.* Revised edition. Maryknoll, N.Y.: Orbis Books, 1994.

Merriman, Brigid O'Shea. *Searching for Christ: The Spirituality of Dorothy Day.* Notre Dame: University of Notre Dame Press, 1994.

Notes

[1] Dorothy Day, *The Long Loneliness* (San Francisco: HarperCollins, 1952), 138.
[2] Ibid., 20.
[3] Ibid., 23–25.
[4] Ibid., 38–39.
[5] Ibid., 50–53.
[6] Ibid., 163–66.
[7] Ibid., 173.
[8] Jim Forest, *Love Is the Measure,* rev. ed. (Maryknoll, N.Y.: Orbis, 1994), 97–99.
[9] Ibid., 111–13.
[10] Ibid., 119.
[11] Dorothy Day, *Dorothy Day: Selected Writings: By Little and By Little,* ed. Robert Ellsberg and Tamar Hennessey (Maryknoll, N.Y.: Orbis, 1992), 80–81.
[12] Ibid., 97–98.
[13] Saint Francis of Assisi, Italy, lived from 1181 to 1226. Although born into considerable wealth, he accepted a life of poverty, much to the chagrin of his father. Francis is remembered for his devotion to preaching, concern for the poor and the sick, and recognition of God's presence in the natural world. The story to which Day refers was a turning point in the religious pilgrimage of Francis. As he was considering God's call to serve the poor, he came upon a begging leper. He was at first horrified by the sight of the man, but stepping forward to give the leper some money, he was filled with compassion and reached out and kissed him.
[14] Dorothy Day, *Loaves and Fishes* (New York: Harper and Row, 1963), 78–79.
[15] Day, *Selected Writings,* 179–80.

CPSIA information can be obtained
at www.ICGtesting.com
Printed in the USA
FFOW01n0314150714
6294FF